Canada's Natives Long Ago

By Donna Ward

Illustrated by Marj Cassidy

DONNA WARD
NORTHWOODS PRESS

Books by Donna Ward:

Canada, My Country (Geography & Social Studies for Early Grades)
Courage and Conquest: Discovering Canadian History (Settlement History for Elementary Grades)
Geography, Province to Province (Canadian Geography for Elementary Grades)
Africa, A Land of Hope (Geography for Elementary Grades)

Cover:
An early 18th century woodland Indian re-enactor, Todd Bitler waits by a trail to get his next plunder. Outfitted in period accoutrements made by Todd, the Shawnee warrior carries goods acquired in the fur trade. Men trapped and hunted for fur and pelts to trade to the whites for such items as wool blankets and yarn, sterling silver, guns, powder horns as well as powder, linen shirts, and more. The whites paid various tribes with these goods during the French and Indian War to fight for control of the continent. Tribes allied with either the French or the British depending on former alliances and trade routes. The most famous Shawnee chief, Tecumseh, died in battle in Upper Canada during the War of 1812. Todd is a living historian and artist. As a native re-enactor and living history teacher he believes that his character must be authentic and believable. Yes, his nose really is pierced through to allow the feather access.
For Todd's website search **Native Workshop** or go through Easylinks at **donnaward.net**

Cover Photograph: Jeff Brown, Corporal, Amherst's 15th Regiment of Foot.
Re-enactors have a passionate love of history and a commitment to help bring it to life.
See Jeff Brown's photographs at **The Kings Company** or go through Easylinks at **donnaward.net.**

Cover Design: Adam Duguay, Images

Printed and Bound in Canada

Revised Editions: 2000, 2004, 2005, 2007
Published by: Donna Ward/Northwoods Press
www.donnaward.net

Canadian Cataloguing in Publication Data

Ward, Donna, 1958-
Canada's natives long ago : for elementary grades

Rev. ed.
ISBN 0-9686788-2-3

1. Indians of North America - Canada - history - Juvenile literature. 2. Inuit - Canada - History - Juvenile literature.
I. Cassidy, Marj, 1929-. II. Title

E89.C2W3672000 971.00497 C00-930713-3

Table Of Contents

Canada's Natives Who are They?

Recommended Resources
Available in most libraries

The following books include information on all the Native groups of Canada and can be used throughout the study. Specific resources are listed at the beginning of each chapter.

This book symbol represents suggested readings in two specific resources as follows:
Native Nations of North America Series: *Life in an Anishinabe Camp; Life in a Longhouse Village; Life in a Plains Camp; Life in the Far North; Native Homes; Nations of the Northwest Coast.* St. Catharines:Crabtree Press, 2001-2003.
Silvey, Diane. *The Kids Book of Aboriginal Peoples.* Toronto: Kids Can Press, 2005. Full colour paintings. An all inclusive Canadian natives book (All grades).

Other Resources:

Beaudry, Lindsay. *Kawin, A Book of Crafts to Do.* Don Mills:Fitzhenry & Whiteside, 1977. An excellent craft book if you can find it in the library.

Dewdney, Selwyn. *They Shared to Survive.* Toronto: MacMillan, 1975. Informative look at Canada's people.

Fisher, Olive and Tyner, Clara L. *Totem, Tipi and Tumpline. Stories of Canadian Indians.* Toronto: J.M. Dent & Sons (Canada) Ltd., 1955. Delightful stories of children, including Native legends (Early and middle grades).

Grant, Bruce. *American Indians Yesterday and Today.* New York: E.P. Dutton & Co. Inc., 1960. An illustrated encyclopedia of Indian terms (All grades).

Holling, C. Holling. *The Book of Indians.* New York: Platt and Munk Co., 1962. In true Holling style, delightful fictional stories designed to teach (All grades).

Hunt, Ben. *The Complete Book of Indian Crafts.* New York: Golden Press, 1954, 1970 (out of print). Excellent projects in authentic form (Middle and upper grades).

Livesey, Robert. *Native Peoples.* Toronto: Stoddart Press., 1992. Includes myths, activities, information. Discovering Canada Series (All grades).

Schemenauer, Elma. *Native Canadians Today and Long Ago.* Scarborough: Nelson Canada, 1985. Easy to read information on Native groups (All grades).

Trottier, Maxine. *Native Crafts, Inspired by North America's First Peoples.* Toronto: Kids Can Press, 2000. Easy to use craft book (All grades).

Getting Ready to Make a Project Book

The student's Natives of Canada project book should include the following:

- ☐ Title page (title, student's name, student's grade or age, date completed).
- ☐ Table of Contents (completed at end of project when pages are numbered).
- ☐ Seven sections for seven cultural groups.
- ☐ Maps (7 copies of p. 4, and 1 copy of each chapter map).
- ☐ Workpages at end of chapters.
- ☐ Project Pictures at end of book.
- ☐ Folder or envelope for storage of pictures until used.

Early grade students should just classify the project pictures. Middle grade children could label and write notes with pictures. Older grade students may add research notes and a bibliography.

Beginnings

Civilization began in a place called the Fertile Crescent in eastern Asia, the area between the Mediterranean Sea and the Persian Gulf. See if you can find this on a map or globe. People groups spread from the Fertile Crescent to all the continents of the world. It is likely that the first Natives of the Americas followed wild game from Asia into Alaska across the Bering Strait. Find this narrow water passage on your globe.

Over thousands of years, the population flourished and grew as the people moved down to occupy both North and South America. The last group to migrate from Asia stayed in the Arctic. They are the Inuit, a people distinct from the natives of the south. People of similar appearance and customs still live on the Siberian shore in Asia.

Inuit of the Central Arctic

Native people were the first or original inhabitants of the Americas. People who are the first to occupy any land are called aborigines of that land. The native people call themselves the First Nations, having existed in North America long before any white people.

When the explorer, Christopher Columbus, first met the inhabitants of North America, he mistakenly thought he had landed in India and called them Indians. They now prefer to be called natives or First Nations.

North American Native

As the aboriginal people spread out across the land, their lifestyle changed in response to the resources of the land. Since there were no stores to buy things, their food, clothing, houses, and tools all had to be made from the plants or animals the land provided. Although tribes varied in language and customs, their culture was similar to other aborigines of the same geographic area. The natives of Canada have thus been categorized into seven cultural groups.

Original: *first, beginning*
Inhabitants*: those living in a land*
Aboriginal*: first dwellers in any land*

Religion

The magnificent sun rose every morning on Canada's natives long ago, warming the earth and sustaining life. The seasons came and went in a rhythm that brought both abundance and need to animals and man. Storms hurled thunderbolts and whipped up waves. Salmon returned mysteriously to the rivers. All the effects of the weather and animal behaviour were felt intimately by the natives, who lived dependently on the cycle of the seasons.

Native spiritual traditions were passed down orally through the generations. It was taught that all living things and objects have spirits and should be respected. The power of life, thinking, and action existed in everything. For instance, the corn goddess was believed to be present in every kernel of corn and able to cause crops to grow or fail depending on her pleasure with the tribe. Behind each storm was the rain god who might be satisfied with a rain ceremony and thus send showers to the thirsty ground. Bones of the salmon were returned to the river in hopes of releasing the spirit of the salmon to ensure that it returned again the next year.

Many tribes sent their adolescents on a vision quest in search of a guiding spirit or vision. Usually the youngster would go to a lonely place and fast (eat no food) for three to four days. During this time they hoped for a vision or dream which might come in the form of an animal spirit. This spirit was then thought to become their lifelong spiritual helper.

Spiritual powers were called medicine. A person with good medicine received favour and safety in life. Medicine bundles were special items carried in a pouch which were considered to have power. Poles were often placed around a camp to hold medicine bundles, enemy scalps, or such things as buffalo horns which were thought to ward off evil. An enemy approaching would be afraid of the spiritual powers of the medicine bundles and so the bundle would, in fact, protect the inhabitants.

Men or women with special power were called shamans. They healed the sick, gave guidance in hunting, and wisdom in war. Natives believed that those who died would go to a new earth where hunting was easy and game plentiful.

Some tribes promoted torture, believing this would gain them favour with the gods. The young warriors of the plains would pierce their skin with skewers during the annual Sun Dance festival. The Iroquois tormented captives thinking that this would bring strength and power to their own tribe. The Natives of the Pacific Coast sometimes sacrificed slaves in their religious ceremonies.

The majority of native tribes were bound to the code of revenge. If a member of their family was killed they believed the soul would not rest until one of the enemy died in payment. Even a man who abhorred killing would be hounded by guilt to avenge his dead.

In today's culture, native spiritual leaders–elders and shamans–encourage aboriginal Canadians to return to their spiritual traditions which no longer include revenge killings, but healing rituals, pow-wow celebrations, and vision quests among others.

The journey of life, or circle of life is

symbolized by the shaman's medicine wheel. The east, direction of the daily birth of the sun, represents a child's birth. The south represents childhood and intellectual growth. The west symbolizes adulthood and deeper thought. The north represents the elder phase of life. The center of the wheel represents Mother Earth.

Native religion is sometimes compared to Hinduism, as both speak of the circle of life. In Hinduism, however, the reference is to reincarnation. Hinduism is one of the world's oldest religions, and the primary religion of India, after whom North Americans were erroneously named.

Hindus believe in *samsara,* a continuing cycle of birth, life, death, and rebirth through many lifetimes. *Karma,* the sum of a person's good and bad deeds, determines how the person will live their next life. Through pure acts, thoughts, and devotion, a person may be reborn at a higher level, while bad deeds incur the opposite. Being reborn as an animal would be the lowest level of life. Wealth or poverty; prestige or suffering are considered the result of previous acts in the present or past lives.

To cause suffering to any living creature is considered abhorrent and wrong. Many Hindus are vegetarians and attempt throughout life never to kill a single creature, even an insect, for it may be someone's mother, father, brother, or sister. The greatest goal of all life is to be released from samsara and reach a state of enlightenment.

Christianity, another major world religion, influenced native culture as missionaries, both Roman Catholic and protestant, came to bring a message of God's love to the aboriginal nations. The foundation of the Christian faith is salvation through the death and resurrection of Jesus Christ, the divine Son of God. Christians believe that there is one God who created all things. Man, being made in God's image, is endowed with power to think, reason, and speak complicated languages. It is man's job to look after the animals and safeguard the earth which God created, rather than animal spirits caring for human beings.

Unfortunately, many so-called Christian Europeans did not practice the principle of love for mankind and the environment. Greed caused both the exploitation of the native peoples and the resources of the land. Greed also caused the native hunters to harvest the land beyond what was needed for personal survival, using animal furs as a means to obtain firearms, pots and knives, beads, and alcohol.

There has been much criticism regarding the effect of missionary efforts on native culture. With prideful hearts some came hoping to change the natives into Europeans rather than bringing the message of God's love. Many others, however, came with sincere hearts and godly convictions. They gave a message of forgiveness instead of revenge, and an understanding of science and medicine to challenge superstition.

Project Book

Begin brainstorming what type of paper and binding method you will use to make a project book. There should be seven sections. Secure copies of the project pictures from the back of the book, cut apart, and store in a file folder. You may alternately choose to make an electronic book using a software program such as PowerPoint.

Meeting the Europeans

The natives of Canada learned to survive with resources from the land. Knives and arrowheads were made of chipped stone. Pots were made of clay, animal skins, or bark. It was a very difficult job securing enough food for everyone and enough skins for clothing. When trade began with the Europeans, the natives acquired metal knives and cooking pots, and most importantly, guns! Hunters using bows and arrows had to slip in very close to an animal and shoot with great strength and accuracy. Guns were far more effective. Firearms revolutionized the lives of natives across Canada. Not only was hunting easier and more successful, but the owners of guns had a much greater advantage against their enemies.

Warring between tribes escalated as the natives were provided with guns. They were drawn into European battles over who would control North America. When Champlain started the first French settlement on the St. Lawrence River, it seemed best to align his men with the Algonkians and Hurons, as they had access to the superior furs. He was obligated to show his friendship by joining them in a raid on their enemies, the Iroquois. Little did Champlain know however, that the French would be plagued for many generations. His actions succeeded in turning the fiercest and most unified tribes of the eastern woodlands against the French.

Prior to meeting the white man, the natives hunted only to provide food and clothing for their people, but their desire for European goods caused them to over hunt in competition with neighbouring tribes. David Thompson, the greatest map maker in Canadian history, penned the following words in 1793.

> The Nepissings, the Algonquins and Iroquois Indians having exhausted their own countries, ...and as they destroyed the Beaver, moved forwards to the northward and westward....For several years all these Indians were rich, the women and children, as well as the men were covered with silver broaches, ear-rings, wampum, beads and other trinkets....The canoes of the fur-traders were loaded with packs of beaver,....Every intelligent man saw the poverty that would follow the destruction of the beaver, but there were no chiefs to control it; all was perfect liberty and equality. Four years afterwards almost the whole of these extensive countries were denuded of beaver, the natives became poor, and with difficulty procured the first necessities of life, and in this state they remain, and probably forever. A worn out field may be manured, and again made fertile; but the beaver, once destroyed cannot be replaced: they were the gold coin of the country, with which the necessaries of life were purchased.[1]

[1] David Thompson. *David Thompson's Narrative.* ed. J.B. Tyrrell (Toronto: the Champlain Society, 1916; reprint ed., New York: Greenwood Press Pub., 1968), p. 255.

The buffalo were first hunted on the plains to provide food, clothing and shelter. Desire for European goods transformed the hunt to increased warfare with other tribes. "The tribes that jostled together on this amazing hunting ground combined the buffalo chase with ceaseless wars, and raided each other for firearms, horses, and scalps until the whole area from the Rockies to the Great lakes became a perpetual battlefield."[1]

The depletion of fur-bearing animals and the push west by settlers in search of farmland left the natives with no hunting ground. In the United States, Indians fought fiercely to retain their lands, losing bitter battles to American soldiers. Eventually, the natives of the USA and Canada were forced to make their homes on *reserves,* land allotted for their use only.

> *In Canada, land allotted for specific native groups are called reserves. In the United States these lands are called reservations.*

The Canadian government and the natives, anxious to avoid war, made agreements called *treaties*. The natives, resigned to the eventual loss of their lands, surrendered their rights in exchange for reserves, money, food, medicine, and other necessities. Treaty promises such as 'your people will never be hungry as long as the river flows and the sun shines,' were promises that were not kept. Many bands were pushed off their lands without treaties.

The natives today who belong to groups that made *treaties* are called *Status Indians.* They have the right to live on their band's reserve and have access to federal government funding for such things as housing and education. They are recognized as a distinct group of people through the Indian Act of 1876.

The natives whose ancestors made no treaties are called *Non-status Indians*. They do not receive the same favours extended to Status Indians. They acquire services such as education and medical insurance through the provincial governments.

[1] Diamond Jenness, *The Indians of Canada.* (Bulletin 65, Anthropological Series No. 15, National Museum of Canada, 1932; reprinted Ottawa: Minister of Supply and Services, Canada, 1977), p. 256.

Project Book
Design a title page for the front cover of your project book. Be creative, neat and colourful. Include a title, your name, grade or age, and the date.

Natives of Today

The problem of the Canadian native in contemporary society is complicated. In many cases, reserves are located in remote northern parts of the provinces where few jobs are available. Without hope of a future career, children are not interested in education. The hopelessness leads to further problems such as suicide, drug and alcohol abuse, and family abuse.

In spite of struggles, each year many native students do enrol in universities. Some bands have started their own businesses such as tourist camps, stores, farming, the sale of native art, and fishing.

The goal of the Indian Act of 1876 was twofold: first, to protect the natives, and secondly, to "civilize" them so that they would eventually move out to find their own homes and jobs among other Canadians. These two goals worked against each other; for the reserve on which they were protected also separated the natives from the people with whom they were supposed to be integrated. Natives were taught farming, children in schools were not allowed to speak their native languages, and some traditional ceremonies were banned.

The native people on the reserves were not happy! Many were living in poverty, resentful of losing their traditional ways. By 1950, the government decided a new Indian Policy was needed. The native people were encouraged to relearn their own unique ways of life, culture, and language.

The white government workers on reserves gradually transferred their authority to native leaders. Government money was provided for native leaders to organize political groups.

In the 1960's, with this fresh sense of identity and regained personal power, many Indian bands began to make land claims. They felt lands had been unjustly taken, or government promises had not been kept. In the 1980's and 1990's more forceful groups made demands, set up roadblocks, and clashed with police. As the First Nations of Canada, some native people believe they do not have to follow Canadian laws but have the right to govern themselves. There are many difficulties attached to native issues today.

Project Book

Get everything ready to begin putting your project book together by gathering the paper (about 4 pages for each of 7 sections), maps, pictures and workpages. Trim the copies of the maps. Put all the project pictures and maps together in your storage envelope or folder.

Inuit of the Arctic

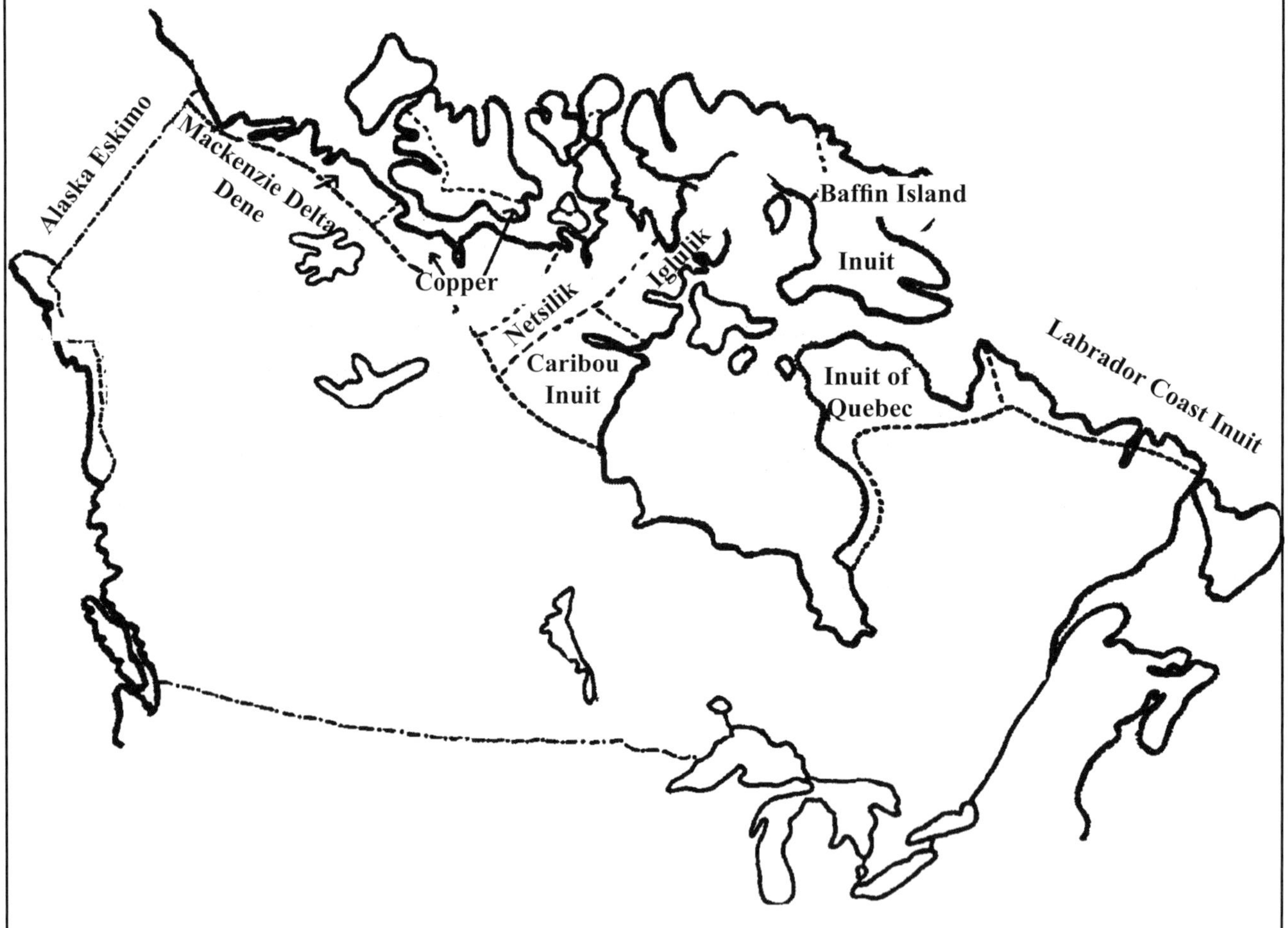

Recommended Resources

Available in most libraries

Aglukark, Susan. *This Child.* (CD or Cassette) Mississauga: EMI Music Canada, 1995.

Alexander, Bryan and Cherry. *Inuit.* Hove, England: Wayland Pub., 1992.

Alexander, Bryan and Cherry. *The Inuit: Hunters of the North.* England: Bramley Books. 1973. Oversize book. Beautiful photographs of present-day Inuit at work & play.

Flaherty, Robert J. *Nanook of the North.* Calif.: Criterion Collection, 1998. Originally filmed in 1922 as a silent motion picture. A classic must-see! (Video/DVD).

George, Jean Craighead. *Julie of the Wolves.* New York: Harper & Row Pub., 1972. Lost on the tundra in Alaska, an Eskimo girl survives with the help of wolves (Novel, All grades).

Haslam, Andrew and Parsons, Alexandra. *Make it Work: Arctic Peoples.* Toronto: Stoddart Pub. Co. Ltd., 1996. Excellent crafts and activities.

Jenness, Aylette and Rivers, Alice. *In Two Worlds: A Yup'ik Eskimo Family.* Boston: Houghton Mifflin Co., 1989. Story of a real family with photographs.

Kalman, Bobbie. *Life in the Far North.* St. Catharines: Crabtree Press, 2001. Native Nations of North America Series well worth having on your bookshelf (All grades).

Kalman, Bobbie. *Native Homes.* St. Catharines: Crabtree Press, 2001. Native Nations of NA (All grades).

Kroll, Virgini*a. The Seasons and Someone.* Florida: Harcourt Brace & Co., 1994. A picture book of an Alaskan girl who witnesses the changing seasons (Early grades).

Marsh, Donald B. *Echoes From a Frozen Land.* Edmonton: Hurtig Publishers, 1987. Story of the Caribou Eskimo by an Anglican minister. (Upper grades).

Marsh, Winifre Petchey. *People of the Willow.* Toronto. Oxford University Press. 1976. Watercolour paintings of the Caribou Eskimo, painted during her years in the north.

National Film Board of Canada. *Kamik.* 1989. An expert hunter & seamstress makes a pair of seal skin boots called Kamik (Video).

National Film Board of Canada. *Inuit–the People*, 1980. Enhanced Filmstrip-on-video.

National Film Board of Canada. *Netsilik Eskimo I.* 1972. Last Inuit group to winter on sea ice. Highly recommended for all ages (Video).

Raine, David F. Pitseolak. *A Canadian Tragedy.* Edmonton: Hurtig Publishers, 1980. A moving story of a young Baffin Island Inuk caught between two cultures (Upper grades).

Pitseolak, Peter. *People From Our Side.* Edmonton: Hurtig Publishers, 1975. Life story with photographs by Baffin Island Inuk, Peter Pitseolak, born in 1902 (Upper grades).

Pitseolak, Peter. *My Escape From Death.* Toronto: McClelland and Stewart, 1977. Peter draws pictures of his experience while lost on a hunting trip (Early grades).

Silvey, Diane. *The Kids Book of Aboriginal Peoples.* Toronto: Kids Can Press, 2005. Great information and full colour paintings. An all inclusive Canadian book (All grades).

Wallace, Mary. *The Inuksuk Book.* Toronto: Owl Books, 1999. A favourite (All grades).

First Kill

"Ashevak" my mother shouted. "Ashevak wake up!" She shook me urgently. What was wrong? I heard the dogs barking. What a noise! So dark! My heart jumped when I remembered all the men had gone away walrus hunting. Only the women and children were left. I was still young and had not often used a gun.

My mother was putting on her parka. Something was outside. She wanted me to go with her. I knew from the sound of the dogs it was something bad. It could be wolves, or a bear, or perhaps some spirit monster!

I was so scared I was shaking. I pulled my parka and boots on at the same time, and scurried through the tunnel to the night outside. It was so dark! There were no stars, or moon, only clouds and darkness. I ran across the brook to catch up with my mother and some others.

"Ashevak!" cried my brother's wife, "Where is your boot?" I stopped to look. I had forgotten one of my boots without even knowing. Now I really shivered.

"Come, come!" yelled my mother. "It is a polar bear after the meat."

Like a blast, the smell of rotten meat hit me. The wind was blowing the smell over us. Then we saw it against the horizon, a huge he-bear. It was clawing and tearing away at the dogs' rotten meat in the cache.

The night was so dark I could hardly see the gun as I knelt to shoot it. Even if my arms were not shaking, it would have been hard to kill the bear, for I could not see down the barrel of the gun. I shot! The bear ran away. My mother and I watched until we could not see it any more, and we went back home.

I climbed back into bed and slowly warmed up. It was a very bad thing to go out without my boot on. I never slept. As soon as dawn came, I hurried out. It was light out now; so, I wasn't afraid, even though I was by myself.

There he was! He had come back to eat at the cache. The bear was down in a hollow; so, I had to go very close. If I missed, the shot would scare him away, but if I injured him, he could charge. The stench of rotten meat enveloped me, but this was good, for the wind did not carry my scent to the bear.

I crouched down and very carefully aimed at that big, old head. The bear was greedily ripping at the meat. Boom! I shot him. He fell down instantly. That was my very first polar bear. I was fifteen years old.

Based on a true story.[1]

[1] Peter Pitseolak. *People From Our Side.* (Edmonton: Hurtig Publishers Ltd., 1975), p. 100.

The People

> If there's one word that says more about the Arctic than any other, certainly it's the word "snow." *This* is the Arctic; indeed, the snow is a sight I'll always remember and treasure - a snow-covered wilderness inhabited by the Eskimos, the bravest people on earth.[1]

Canadians have always identified themselves as hardy people enduring, and even frolicking in a winter-bound land. Most of us, however, live in a narrow strip along the southern border. The true northern dwellers, the Inuit of the Arctic, have long held the fascination of Canadians in the south. They have become symbols of endurance and ingenuity as they survive and even prefer their harsh Arctic homeland.

Howling winds and blinding blizzards are two of the many hardships of Canada's 'great white north' where snow and ice reign for ten out of twelve months. Midwinter days are dreary and dark; the sun never showing its cheerful glow. As spring comes, the days quickly get longer until finally, the sun doesn't set, but lingers on the horizon and then rises again in "the Land of the Midnight Sun."

Above the treeline, the few trees look like low stunted bushes although they may be many years old, for the growing season is short. In most of the arctic, the *permafrost* allows only mosses, berries and wild flowers to survive.

Long before the white man came, the Inuit wrestled a living from the frozen sea or barren tundra. As fuel was scarce, meat was most often eaten raw. Thus these people became known as *Eskimos*, a southern native term meaning "eaters of raw meat." In 1977, the Arctic Eskimos in Canada agreed to adopt the name *Inuit*, meaning "the people." One person is called an *Inuk*. Inuit speak a common language called *Inuktitut*.

> ***permafrost**: ground permanently frozen just below the surface*

Over the past century, the lifestyle of the Inuit has changed drastically and they have faced many struggles as they adapt to new ways. Positions of authority in the arctic lands were often in the hands of people from the south. The Arctic Inuit are now seeking to regain control over their land and lives. In April, 1999, Canada's third territory was formed from part of the Northwest Territories. It is governed by the Inuit and is called *Nunavut* (pronounced Noon-a-vut) meaning "our land."

---

[1] Donald Marsh, *Echoes From a Frozen Land.* (Edmonton: Hurtig Publishers Ltd., 1987), p. 95.

📖 *Life in the Far North,* pp. 4-11.

Project Book
Make a title page for the Inuit of the Arctic section. It should be page 3 of your project book after the main title page and the Table of Contents which you will complete later.

Food

For the majority of Inuit groups the sea provided most of what they needed to survive. The small ringed seal, which lives under the sea ice, could be harpooned throughout the winter. The seal supplied them with food, oil for heating and cooking, and hides for boots, clothing, and tents. Walrus and whales were also hunted.

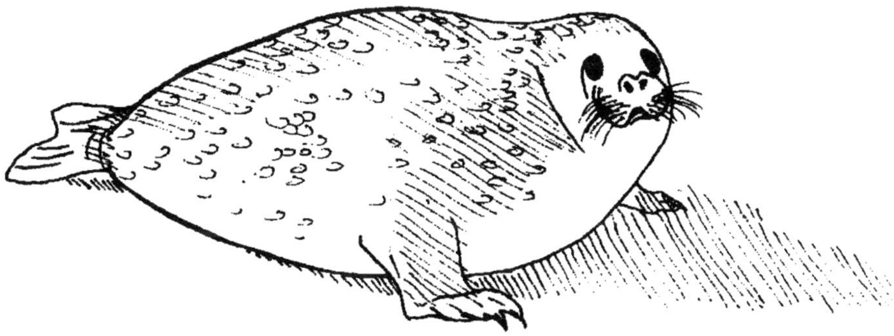

The most valuable land mammal was the caribou. In the fall, hunters intercepted the caribou on their southern migrations. At this time, caribou hides were in their best condition and suitable for winter clothing.

For some inland groups on either side of Hudson Bay, caribou meat was a main winter staple. Other sources of food were the muskox, polar bear, waterfowl and ptarmigan. Birds' eggs, and a few berries and plants provided variety. Most of the food was eaten raw, because without wood, there was little fuel for cooking.

Food was stored in a *cache*, a hole in the frozen ground. Rocks piled on top, kept it safe from marauding wolves or bears. In the summer, meat was dried to preserve it, though sometimes decaying meat was preferred.

Cache: *a secure place for storing food or tools*

Some of the foods preferred by the Inuit of long ago, such as blood soup, raw liver, or the partially digested stomach contents of a caribou, seem repulsive to us. However, they contained the nutrition the Inuit needed to stay healthy on a diet that did not include fruits or vegetables.

...one delicacy called for a whole sealskin, complete with the blubber layer, to be stuffed with small sea birds and left under rocks until the contents had turned to the consistency of cheese.[1]

[1] Alan D. McMillan, *Native Peoples and Cultures of Canada.* (Vancouver: Douglas & McIntyre, 1988), p.254.

Life in the Far North, pp. 12-15; *Kids Book of Aboriginal Peoples*, pp. 26-27.

Project Book
Colour the correct project picture of the food of this cultural group. Draw additional pictures and/or write things you learned about the food and the gathering of it. Glue notes and pictures in your project book.

Shelter

The Inuit are an incredible people known for their resourcefulness in using what nature provides. In past days, they used what was available from the land to make secure homes.

The Mackenzie Delta Dene, in the western Northwest Territories, lived in igloos which were partially underground. Poles laid across the top of the walls and draped with skins formed the roof. Then the first winter storm covered and insulated the home with snow.

It was the Inuit of the central region who lived in an *igloo* made entirely of snow blocks. The entrance was a tunnel leading to a snow porch which provided storage space. Here the outer clothing was brushed off and left. The tunnel then continued on to the interior of the home.

In the igloo, caribou skins draped over platforms of snow served as beds and seats. The only heat was a small soapstone lamp, which burned smoky whale or seal oil, therefore the temperature in the igloo rarely rose above the freezing point. Inside, people stayed dressed in their inner parkas; however, babies were allowed to romp naked for short periods, impervious to the cold.

When the snow began to melt, the Inuit moved into tents made with frames of whale bones or driftwood and covered in animal skins. Donald Marsh, missionary to the Inuit, remembers spring in the Arctic.

> Spring is a wonderful time in the Arctic. The sun actually begins to feel warm and the snow starts to melt.... I recall a three o'clock morning visit from a family who burst into our home laughing hard because the igloo roof had fallen on top of them in bed. The next day they erected a tent shelter within the igloo as the final stage before moving out.[1]

The people groups of the west, around the mouth of the Mackenzie River, lived in large villages, as did the Eastern Inuit of Labrador. Central Inuit were more nomadic, travelling and hunting in small groups in summer and living in larger villages in the winter. These groups often joined their igloos with tunnels to allow easy access for visiting. Inuit people love to socialize.

[1] Ibid., pp. 37,39.

Life in the Far North, pp. 18-21; *Kids Book of Aboriginal Peoples*, pp. 24-25.

Project Book
Colour the correct project picture of the housing of this cultural group. On lined paper write different things you learned about their shelters. Glue the notes and the picture in your project book.

Moving and Hunting

The Inuit had two types of boats for travel. The one-man *kayak,* the most ingenious aboriginal boat, could slip through the water quickly and silently. The larger *umiak* was able to carry big loads such as whale meat and blubber, or a family and their goods moving to an Arctic island. Both boats were made of sealskin stretched over frames of whalebone or driftwood.

Families travelling across the land in the summer packed loads on their dogs and carried everything else on their own backs.

Travel was easier when snow and ice covered the land. Loads could be pulled on dog sleds called *komatiks.* In the west, where there were more trees, dogs were harnessed in pairs or one behind the other since the trails were narrow. When travelling on the open tundra, sled dogs were harnessed in a fan-shaped pattern.

The Arctic people had to travel to find food. On the sea, walrus, seal, and whale were hunted. Caribou were easier prey when they swam across lakes or inlets. The people knew the best locations to find food.

In summer, some Inuit groups hunted whales. Sealskins were tied and blown up like balloons and then attached to the ends of harpoons as floats. The hunter would manoeuvre his kayak close enough to the whale to thrust a harpoon into it. The floats dragged behind it and slowed it down. When it was exhausted, the whale surfaced and the hunters killed it with harpoons. A favourite treat, especially for the children, was raw whale blubber.

In the winter, the dogs' keen sense of smell helped the hunter search for seal breathing holes. Seals surface for air three or four times every hour. The hunter prodded through the snow with his harpoon to find the hole, and then carefully dug away the snow to expose it. A feather placed at the hole fluttered when the seal came to breath. A hunter stood motionless watching the feather closely, possibly for many hours, until a seal came to breath. Then he thrust his harpoon down the hole to kill the seal. Meat from a seal could feed a group for several days.

Life in the Far North, pp. 16-17; *Kids Book of Aboriginal Peoples*, p. 28.

Project Book
Colour the correct project picture of the method of transportation of this cultural group. Add some notes and glue notes, project picture and any additional material or pictures in your project book.

Work and Customs

The Inuit generally lived in close family units, with sometimes just one or two families together. When the hunting was good, large groups would gather. People passed the long winter hours with games and storytelling. The Inuit were, and still are, very sociable, always visiting and laughing together.

Survival depended upon sharing as a community. Any successful hunter shared the prize with the whole camp. Tools, food from a cache or recent kills were all shared.

While the men hunted, the women spent many hours preparing hides and sewing clothing. Inner clothing and leggings of caribou hide were worn next to the skin with the fur facing outward. The outer parka was designed with the fur facing inward toward the body. Warm, waterproof sealskin boots protected their feet. Women and girls chewed the hides to soften them. Sometimes boots had to be rechewed if they had hardened.

Babies stayed cosy in their mother's *aumiat*, a hood-like pouch of the mother's parka. Wearing only a hat, a child might stay in the pouch up to three years before his first set of clothing was made. Parents dearly loved their children, but if a mother gave birth while she still had a baby in her *aumiat*, a relative would adopt the new baby since there was only room for one to stay warm in the mother's hood.

Life in the Far North, pp. 22-31; *Kids Book of Aboriginal Peoples*, pp. 29.

Project Book

Using a copy of the map from page 4, colour the correct location of this cultural group. Using a copy of the Inuit of the Arctic map, colour the locations of the different tribes of this cultural group. Add the maps to your project book.

Susan Aglukark
Arctic Rose

I was told I was a dreamer
Wanting things I couldn't have
And Daddy here I am
Singing my song, singing my dreams for you.
Lyrics from "Dreams For You," Aglukark.

The daughter of an Inuit Pentecostal preacher, Susan discovered a love for singing in the choir of her father's church in Arviat, on the western shore of Hudson Bay. She grew up firmly rooted in the Christian faith.

There were times when Susan's faith was severely tested. While attending high school in Iqluit on Baffin Island, NWT, she felt an overwhelming pressure to experiment with drugs and alcohol. To get away, Susan spent three months at Bible School in Cambridge Bay, NWT. Eventually, Susan did graduate from high school in Yellowknife and then began a career as a translator for the Department of Indian Affairs and Northern Development in Ottawa.

While there, Susan made her first tentative step into the music industry by releasing a gospel cassette with the help of CBC Radio. Later, with her manager and Bible School friend, Val Haas, Susan independently produced the album *Arctic Rose.* Selling an impressive 15,000 copies, the album caught the attention of a Canadian record company who signed a contract with Susan to produce six more albums. The first album, *This Child*, was released in January, 1995.

Susan's high school yearbook said her goal was to be the first Inuk to win a major musical award. She has since received three Juno awards, which are Canada's top musical awards. The Order of Canada—Canada's highest civilian honour—was awarded to Susan in 2005 for her contribution both musically and as a workshop facilitator and mentor in the aboriginal community.

Susan has realized her dream, but more importantly, she has a mission to urge young people, especially Inuit young people, to stay in school, reject the use of drugs and to reach for their dreams.

www.susanaglukark.com

Activities

To pass long winter hours, the Inuit played many games. Two of their favourites were Cat's Cradle, a string game, and Nooglooktok, a game requiring the coordination and skill needed in hunting. You can try your skill at either game.

Cat's Cradle:

Gryski, Camilla. *Many Stars & More String Games.* Toronto: Kids Can Press. 1985.
Gryski, Camilla. *Favourite String Games.* Toronto: Kids Can Press. 1995.

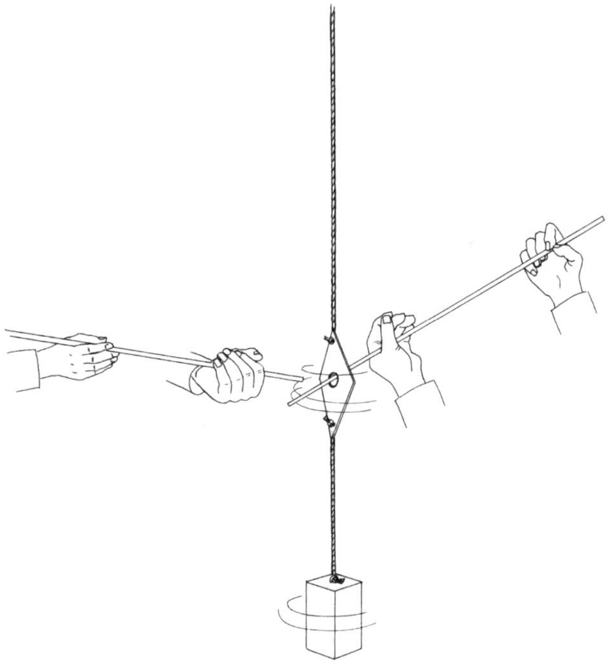

Nooglooktok:

Getting Ready

1. The Inuit used an oblong piece of bone drilled with a hole, but you can use a piece of cardboard or wood about 15 cm long. Cut it in a diamond shape; put a 4 cm hole in the centre and a small hole in each end.
2. Tie a long string through the hole in one end and suspend it outside from a tree limb, or inside, perhaps from a pole on the backs of two chairs. The Inuit would set up a tripod with tent poles to suspend the game piece.
3. On the other end, hang a heavy object as a weight.

Playing the Game

Each person should have in hand a piece of dowelling or a straw, which imitates a lance used in hunting.

The object of the game is to be the first to spear the hole while the game piece is spinning. The more often players hit the object, the more it should spin. This game would be played by the hour in the igloo in the winter, or outdoors in the summer.

Vocabulary

permafrost	*Nunavut*	*umiak*
Eskimo	*igloo*	*komatik*
Inuit, Inuk	*cache*	*aumiat*
Inuktitut	*kayak*	*Juno Award*

Inuit of the Arctic Workpage

Draw lines to match the word to its definition.

aumiat	a place to store food or tools
igloo	a large skin boat
cache	one person of Inuit descent
kayak	a dog sled
permafrost	the hood in a mother's parka for carrying a baby
umiak	a one-man skin boat
komatik	an Inuit house of snow blocks
Inuk	ground permanently frozen below the surface

Complete this page and add it to your project book.

Eastern Woodland Farmers

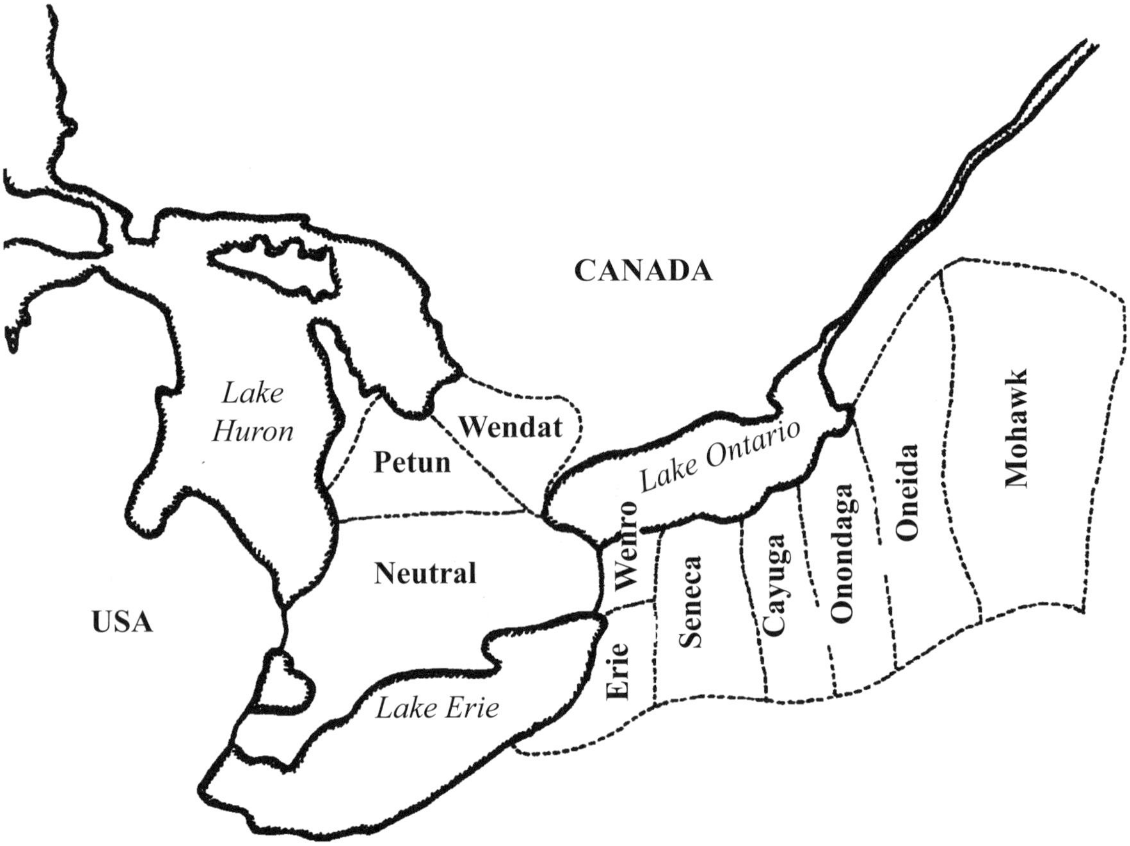

Recommended Resources

Available in most libraries

Beaudry, Lindsay. Kawin, *A Book of Crafts to Do*. Don Mills: Fitzhenry & Whiteside, 1977. An excellent craft book if you can find it in the library.

Brebeauf, Father Jean de. *The Huron Carol.* Toronto: Key Porter Kids. 1990. Huron Christmas carol with beautiful illustrations (Picture Book).

Cass, James. *Ekahotan, the Corn Grower*. Toronto: Heath Canada Ltd. & the Royal Ontario Museum, 1983. Good information with colour pictures (All grades).

D'Amato, Janet and Alex. *Indian Crafts*. Toronto: George J. McLeod Ltd., 1968.

D'Amato, Janet and Alex. *Algonquian and Iroquois Crafts For You to Make.* New York: Simon and Schuster, 1979.

Holling, C. Holling. *The Book of Indians.* New York: Plat & Munk Co., 1962, Chapters 2-4. In true Holling style, delightful fictional stories designed to teach (All grades).

Kalman, Bobbie. *Life in a Longhouse Village*. St. Catharines: Crabtree Press, 2001. Native Nations of North America Series well worth having on your bookshelf (All grades).

Kalman, Bobbie. *Native Homes*. St. Catharines: Crabtree Press, 2001. Native Nations of North America Series (All grades).

Junior Encyclopedia of Canada, 1990 ed., S.V. "Huron." Edmonton: Hurtig Publishers, 1990. Excellent full page drawing of life in a Huron village.

Lenski, Lois. *Indian Captive, The Story of Mary Jemison*. New York: Harper Trophy, 1941, 1995. An outstanding fictionalized biography of a New England captive who chose to remain with the Iroquois. Good read-aloud novel (All grades).

Monture, Ethel Brant. *Famous Indians.* Toronto: Clarke, Irwin & Co. Ltd., 1960. Well-told story of Joseph Brant by his great-great-granddaughter (Middle & upper grades).

Patterson, Nancy-Lou and Palmer. *Iroquoians of the Eastern Woodlands.* Toronto: Grolier Ltd., 1985.

Petrie, Roy A. *Joseph Brant.* Don Mills: Fitzhenry & Whiteside Ltd., 1978 (Upper grades).

Ridington, Jillian and Robert. *People of the Longhouse.* Vancouver: Douglas & McIntyre Ltd., 1982.

Silvey, Diane. *The Kids Book of Aboriginal Peoples.* Toronto: Kids Can Press, 2005. Great information and full colour paintings. An all inclusive Canadian book (All grades).

Video Collection. *Hurons: Indians of North America*. Pennsylvania: Schlessinger Video Productions, 1995. Documentary about the French speaking Hurons of Lorette.

The Ever Present Enemy

"Caw! Caw! shouted the boys as they flapped their arms at the crows who threatened the ripe corn. Slow Turtle yawned. He had been on the platform all afternoon, frustrating his friends by enjoying the sun more than guarding the corn.

"Get moving, slow one," someone nudged. Slow Turtle slipped off the platform and yawning again, found a warm patch of dirt hidden by corn stalks. He curled up for an undisturbed nap.

Many hours later, the chill of the evening air awakened Slow Turtle. He had been dreaming of whispers and bird calls. Wait! That was a real voice! Fully alert, Slow Turtle lay motionless, listening. Silently, in the dusky light, two shadows moved through the corn. Enemies!

Slow Turtle waited until the figures had passed and then, heart pounding, he crept cautiously toward the village. These summer raiding parties were usually small, five to seven warriors. They would wait until the camp was sleeping, therefore, there was still time for a warning. But how could a boy cross the open ground unseen?

Slowly, silently, Slow Turtle crawled through the stalks. Then an idea came to him. If he could get to the river bank unseen, he would boldly walk right into the village, as if from fishing. Would the spies harm him? No! Not unless they caught him in the corn. Slow Turtle shivered at the thought.

Peering furtively in the dim light, Slow Turtle inched towards the river. He strained his ears for every sound, thinking that at any moment he would be pounced upon. There it was, the lapping of the water! Taking a deep breath, Slow Turtle left the cover of the corn and scurried across the open ground towards the river.

Now was the test of his courage! He must not appear anxious. Oh, how he wanted to race to the village, but he forced himself to walk slowly. Did the fear show on his face? He was almost at the gate!

"STOP!" a voice commanded. Shaking, the boy looked up into the frowning face of the village sentry. "No fish again, Slow Turtle? You are a slow no-good! Hurry into the village. It is almost dark."

As he passed the sentry, Slow Turtle whispered, "Enemies in the corn." In no time, word went through the village and the warriors quietly prepared.

Early that night, fires were put out and when the camp seemed at rest, the attack came. The enemy was astonished by the fearsome warriors defending their village. The raiders fled and were chased into the night. All the next day, Slow Turtle was praised. He was given the honour that evening of retelling the victory story.

"Your name is no longer Slow Turtle," stated the chief. "It is Bold Fox, for with cunning and boldness you save your people."

The People

Heavy with sorrow, the chief wandered the forest, mourning the loss of his wife and three daughters because of enemy wars. Usually a man took revenge by killing in return, but Hiawatha[1] was tired of the bloodshed.

At a lake he found beautiful shells. Threading them on strands of grass he said, "If I find anyone full of suffering I will take these shells and comfort them. The strings will become words and carry away their grief. Because I hold the strings in my hand, my words will be true." These shell strings became the first wampum.

Deganawida, another peace seeker, came to Hiawatha. Together they created laws of peace with a string of wampum for each law to help the people remember them. Then they travelled from tribe to tribe, finally persuading the chiefs of five nations to join their Great League of Peace. The five tribes called themselves *Hodenosaunee*, or "People of the Longhouse." Their alliance was strong. They had peace among themselves but were very warlike to outsiders. Others called them the Iroquois, meaning "poisonous snakes."

Another league was that of the Wendat who lived east of Georgian Bay. They were called "Huron" by the French.

These groups, along with a few others, were called Iroquoian, because their language was similar and their lifestyle unique from other cultural groups. In all of Canada, this was the only group of natives who obtained most of their food by farming.

Huron was a French word meaning 'unkempt knave,' or 'poorly kept man of low birth.' The preferable name is Wendat, meaning 'Islanders' or 'Dwellers on the Peninsula.'

[1] Not the Hiawatha of Longellow's poem nor Disney fame.

Life in a Longhouse Village, pp. 4-5.

Project Book
Make a title page for the Eastern Woodland Farmers.

Food

Most Iroquoian food was grown in the ground. The men cleared the field and the women prepared the soil. The three main food crops were corn (sometimes called *maize*), squash, and beans. The people called these foods "the three sisters" and always planted them together.

As plants flourished, the women and children stood on platforms and shooed the birds from the fields. Sentries kept watch against enemies who might set fire to the fields to destroy the food supply.

In the *Month the Corn Became Sweet* (August), the Iroquoians celebrated at the Green Corn Ceremony. Games and songs welcomed the crops that would sustain the people over the barren winter.

When the crops were harvested, the women preserved the food. Corn was ground into corn meal. Husks of corn were braided together and hung from the eaves of the homes to dry. Today we enjoy popcorn which was discovered by native farmers.

Tobacco was also grown. Natives smoked ceremonial pipes and introduced smoking to the Europeans. Offerings of tobacco were thrown on the fire in the hopes of obtaining favour from the spirits.

Along with farming, the Iroquoian people fished, hunted, and gathered berries. This combination of farming, gathering, and hunting provided security, because if the hunting was poor, the crops would sustain the people, or if the harvest failed, fish and meat would still be available.

Life in a Longhouse Village, pp. 12-17; *Kids Book of Aboriginal Peoples*, p. 40.

Project Book
Colour the correct project picture of the food of this cultural group. Draw additional pictures and/or write things you learned about the food and the gathering of it. Add to your project book.

Shelter

Unlike those who lived by hunting, the Eastern Woodland Farmers were able to construct large permanent villages because their food supply never moved away.

However, when the soil stopped producing good crops, the people relocated their villages to a new site.

When houses were needed, the Iroquoian builders erected poles for the frame of the large longhouse. Slabs of elm bark covered the frame. A door was located at each end. The doorway area was often used as a storage porch. If more room was needed, it was easy to build an extension onto the end of the longhouse.

Inside, two platforms ran along the walls of the house. The lower one, covered with skins, was use for the beds. The upper platform became storage space. Braided corn, tobacco leaves, tools and weapons all hung from the eaves.

Smoke drifted up through the holes in the roof from the cooking fires which burned at intervals down the centre of the longhouse. One family lived on either side of the hearth and shared the fire with the other. These large buildings housed ten or more related families. How would you like to live with lots of cousins?

A single village could have up to thirty longhouses. Around the village, a wall of poles, or a palisade, helped protect the homes and people from raiding enemies.

Iroquoian: *All the tribes in the farming cultural group that spoke the Iroquian dialect.*
Iroquois*: The tribes south of Lake Ontario that joined together as "The Five (later, Six) Nations."*

Native Homes, pp. 8-11; *Life in a Longhouse Village,* pp. 6-9; *Kids Book of Aboriginal Peoples*, pp. 36-37.

Project Book
Colour the correct project picture of the housing of this cultural group. On lined paper write different things you learned about their shelters. Glue the notes and the picture in your project book.

Travel and War

Hiawatha may have brought peace among The Five Nations but the Iroquois men were not peaceful. If anything, their alliance made them more powerful against their enemies.

Young men found honour from daring battle feats. Each year, war parties would plan their conquests. Groups of about six would sneak into the territory of their enemies, terrorizing the trails, killing hunters, or kidnapping women and children.

A scalp, hair from the head of a dead enemy, was displayed as a trophy. Sometimes an enemy warrior would be tortured to death, as it was thought that the spirit of his bravery would enter the village and give the people more power.

The first white people in Canada discovered that animal furs brought a high price in Europe. They traded beads, knives, pots, and other goods for furs. Competition among the Iroquoian confederacies grew so strong that eventually the Wendat, Neutral and Tobacco tribes were all killed or scattered.

The native wars became entangled in the French and English struggle for North America. The French were friends with the northern tribes, the Wendat and Algonquins; the British were allies with the Iroquois. In the end, the strength between the Iroquois and English was too much for the French. If the alliances had been different Canada may have been predominantly French today.

The Eastern Woodland farmers travelled mostly on foot. Braves could cover long distances very quickly and silently. They made elm bark canoes, but these were heavy and sluggish compared to the northern birch bark canoe. In more peaceful times, Iroquoians traded corn with northern tribes for goods and birch bark canoes.

During the American Revolution, under the leadership of Joseph Brant, the Iroquois (except the Oneida) fought with the British against the Americans. After the war they were rewarded for their loyalty with tracts of land in Ontario. Joseph Brant received land along the Grand River and created the Six Nations Reserve near the town of Brantford, Ontario, which was named after him.

Life in a Longhouse Village, pp. 18-21.

Project Book
Colour the correct project picture of the method of transportation of this cultural group. Add some notes and glue the notes, project picture and any additional material or pictures in your project book.

Work and Customs

Children born today in Canada usually receive their father's last name, but Iroquoian children took their mother's clan name. This was a matriarchal society. After marriage, a man moved into his wife's longhouse but was responsible to train his sister's children who carried his clan name and were thus considered his descendants more than his own children.

Women were highly respected, especially the clan matron who was the oldest and most capable woman of the family group. She controlled clan decisions such as choosing a chief or distributing food.

In everyday life, men of these farming nations cleared the fields, built houses, went to war and hunted. The women planted, harvested, prepared food and clothing, and looked after the children.

When the men went to trade with other tribes, strings of beads or *wampum*, were sometimes used as money. Wampum strings were also carried to pass messages between tribes. In council meetings of the League of Five Nations, a belt of wampum was held by the speaker to show that his words were true. It was passed on in acceptance of the words and as a signal for the next speaker to begin.

The different villages regularly congregated for festivals where clans were pitted against each other in games of skill and endurance. *Lacrosse*, popular among the Iroquois, could include teams of over 100 men. A ball was caught within the woven basket at the end of a long stick and carried down the field to the goal posts. Lacrosse is now the summer National Sport of Canada.

*A **clan** was a group of related families. A **tribe** was made up of many, many clans, and could include numerous villages.*

Life in a Longhouse Village, pp. 10-11, 24-28; Kids Book of Aboriginal Peoples, pp. 38-39.

Project Book
Using a copy of the map from page 4, colour the correct location of this cultural group. Using a copy of the Eastern Woodland Farmers map, colour the locations of the different tribes of this cultural group. Add the maps to your project book.

Joseph Brant - Thanendanegea

Joseph Brant held a small stick in his mouth and bit down hard in pain. Outwardly, he kept his face as calm as possible. He was thirteen, a warrior heading into battle. He wanted to appear brave and strong but nearly cried out as more hair was plucked from his head. Soon the pain would be over and he would proudly wear his roach hair style as a true Mohawk warrior.

The battle against the French at Lake George (New York State) was exciting and terrifying for the young Mohawk. Although many men were killed, the Iroquois and the British won. William Johnson, the Irishman who had led the battle for the British, was married to Joseph Brant's older sister, Molly. Johnson was the agent for Indian affairs and did his best to help the Iroquois.

As a boy, Joseph had attended a British mission school where he became a Christian. When Johnson needed a business aid, Brant's heritage, schooling and noble manner made him the best candidate. In this position, he gained great diplomatic skill and made important British friendships.

In 1977, during the American Revolution, Joseph Brant led an attack on Fort Hunter. His warriors carried away a child who was returned the next morning with this note: "Sir, I send you by one of our runners the child which we will deliver, that you may know whatever others do, I do not make war on women and children. I am sorry to say that I have those engaged with me in the service, who are more savage than the savages themselves." (Brant refers to British soldiers and the militia.)[1]

Joseph married the daughter of an Oneida chief, but she died early of tuberculosis. He then married her sister, who sadly, also succumbed to the same disease.

When war broke out in 1775, as the Americans revolted against British rule, Brant sailed to England to meet with King George III. Brant promised to keep the Iroquois loyal to England. Most of the tribes followed Joseph, but the Tuscaroras and Oneidas sided with the American colonies.

After the American victory, the British gave all the Iroquois land over to the Americans. Joseph's people were homeless. The Mohawk leader furiously struggled to gain compensation from Britain. Eventually, Brant was given land for his people in Ontario. He founded the Six Nations Reserve and the nearby village of Brant's ford, which is now called Brantford (famous now as the hometown of Wayne Gretsky and Alexander Graham Bell).

For the rest of his life Brant worked tirelessly to improve conditions for his people and to help them adjust to a new way of life.

[1] Virginia Irving Armstrong, *I Have Spoken.* (Chicago: The Swallow Press Inc.), p. 30.

Activities

Native beads were first made from sea shells and used for wampum or decorations on clothing. When the Europeans came, their glass beads used for trade replaced the delicate shell beads. Beaded clothing showed wealth.

Beading:
There are many options for bead craft using seed beads obtained from any craft store. Various methods for beading can be explored using craft books from the library or craft store.

Models:
Make a model longhouse. Use a nail to punch holes in a thick piece of cardboard. Push the ends of flexible branches into the holes; making certain that the branch pieces are all the same length. Use thin wire or string to lash straight, vertical pieces to each flexible frame piece as shown. Cardboard egg cartons can be cut and soaked in brown and black tempera paint to look like elm bark. Place them on the frame like shingles starting at the bottom. They will dry curved. When dry, glue them in place, leaving a smoke hole in the roof. Cut a small piece of brown fabric for the door.

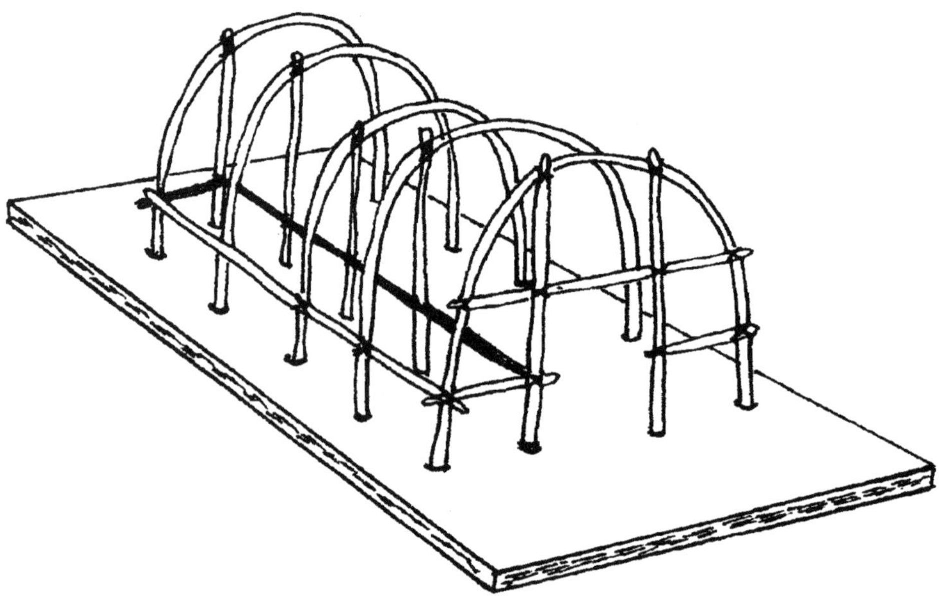

Vocabulary

maize	*palisade*	*matriarchal*
wampum	*lacrosse*	*clan*
Iroquoian	*Iroquois*	*permanent*

Eastern Woodland Farmers Workpage

M	W	A	E	C	M	A	I	Z	E	K	L	S	C	M	P
I	A	S	Q	U	A	S	H	L	E	N	O	M	A	T	R
S	R	O	N	M	E	U	E	P	A	L	I	S	A	D	E
S	A	O	H	W	K	O	Q	U	N	I	R	S	E	I	R
O	I	S	Q	M	T	S	L	A	C	R	O	S	S	E	A
P	O	R	M	U	N	E	H	F	A	R	Q	L	O	T	B
B	M	E	X	Y	O	W	N	E	A	R	U	I	S	E	R
P	O	I	Q	O	R	I	M	T	N	R	O	C	P	H	A
C	H	L	N	E	I	N	S	W	R	I	I	F	B	A	N
W	A	M	P	U	M	Q	H	R	D	G	A	P	A	M	T
L	W	E	N	D	A	T	O	R	E	R	N	T	S	A	V
P	K	S	R	W	E	I	N	T	M	I	O	S	W	C	B
I	P	O	S	S	R	E	M	E	N	C	L	E	N	P	C
H	I	B	U	R	O	S	R	C	E	M	T	R	B	L	D
P	A	T	A	L	O	N	G	H	O	U	S	E	A	P	K
U	I	W	N	D	E	I	P	E	B	E	A	N	S	H	T

Words may be horizontal, vertical, diagonal and backwards.

BEANS
BRANT
CLAN
CORN
FARMER
IROQUOIAN
IROQUOIS
LACROSSE
LONGHOUSE
MAIZE
MOHAWK
PALISADE
SQUASH
WAMPUM
WARRIOR
WENDAT

Complete this page and add it to your project book.

Eastern Woodland Hunters

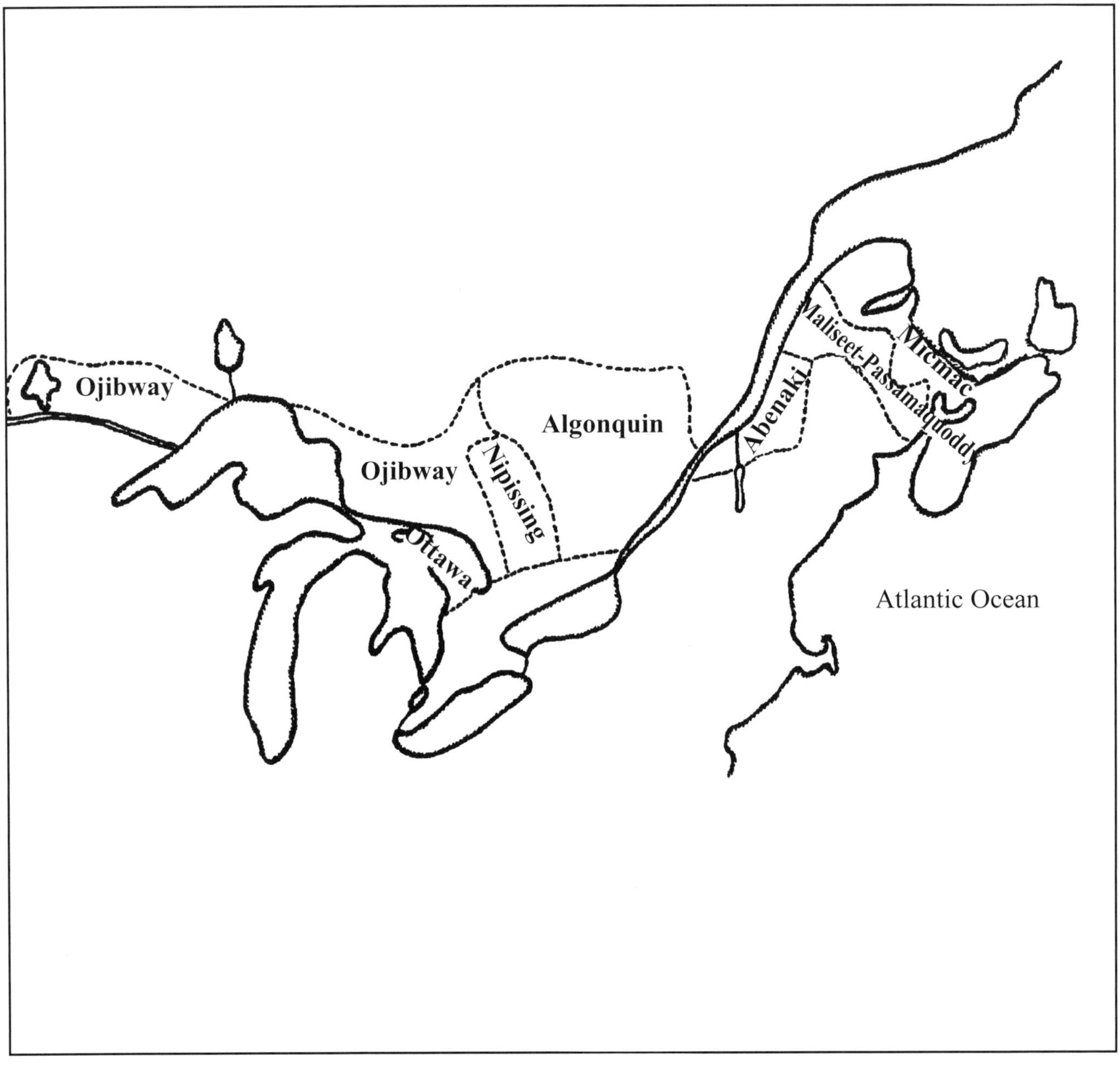

Recommended Resources

Available in most libraries

Beaudry, Lindsay. *Kawin, A Book of Crafts to Do.* Don Mills: Fitzhenry & Whiteside, 1977. An excellent craft book if you can find it in the library.

D'Amato, Janet and Alex. *Algonquian and Iroquois Crafts For You To Make.* New York: Simon and Schuster, 1979. Excellent craft ideas for various ages.

D'Amato, Janet and Alex. *Indian Crafts*. Toronto: George McLeod, Ltd., 1968. Another great craft book for all ages.

Gidmark, David. *The Indian Crafts of William and Mary Commanda.* Toronto: McGraw- Hill Ryerson Ltd., 1980. True Algonquin crafts, such as snowshoes, quillwork, and a birchbark canoe are described and pictured. (Upper grades)

Goller, Claudine. *Algonkian Hunters of the Eastern Woodlands*. Toronto: Grolier Ltd.,1984. Good information with black and white drawings. (Middle to upper grades)

Kalman, Bobbie. *Life in an Anishinabe Camp*. St. Catharines: Crabtree Press, 2003. Native Nations of North America Series well worth having on your bookshelf (All grades).

Kalman, Bobbie. *Native Homes*. St. Catharines: Crabtree Press, 2001. Native Nations of NA (All grades).

Marshall, Ingeborg. *The Red Ochre People.* Vancouver: J.J. Douglas Ltd., 1977. How the Beothuck Indians lived.

Silvey, Diane. *The Kids Book of Aboriginal Peoples.* Toronto: Kids Can Press, 2005. Great information and full colour paintings. An all inclusive Canadian book (All grades).

Speare, Elizabeth. *Sign of the Beaver.* Boston: Houghton Mifflin Co., 1983. The son of a settler learns the ways of a neighbouring native brave (Novel, Middle Grades).

Theriault, Madeline Katt. *Moose to Moccasins. The Story of Ka Kita Wa Pa No Kwe.* Toronto: Natural Heritage/Natural History Inc., 1992. Born in 1908, Madeline learned the old ways from great-grandparents. Told simply, the story brings fascinating insight (All grades).

Time-Life Books. *People of the Lakes.* Virginia: Time-Life Inc., 1994. Excellent photographs of Ojibwa harvesting wild rice and making maple sugar (All grades).

Rabbit Fur's Dream

As a tiny child the little girl loved to snuggle under blankets of rabbit fur and thus she earned her name, Rabbit Fur. Now she was a young woman, almost old enough to be married.

It was the Month of Crushed Leaves (September) when the cranberries were ready. Collecting birch bark baskets, Rabbit Fur set off to find the cranberries growing in the rocky gullies by the beaver pond. Filling one basket, she set it up on the bare rock and scrambled back down to the moss and berry bushes below. Her fingers worked quickly as the sun drew lower behind the trees.

Stepping lightly on a rock, Rabbit Fur cried out as it shifted and sent her tumbling! In dismay, she watched berries roll into rock crevices and disappear. Her disappointment turned to fear, for as she rose to stand she felt her leg buckle under her. After the pain subsided, Rabbit Fur assessed the situation: the dark was almost upon her; her ankle was badly sprained or broken; and no one else knew where this berry patch was. Painfully, Rabbit Fur pulled up moss and scooped cold dirt to pack on her ankle. Finding a few leaves for cover, she pulled her arms inside her deerskin dress and burrowed down, shivering, for a night of fitful sleep. In her troubled dreams, Rabbit Fur saw a mother beaver waddle close to cover and protect her with its large, flat tail.

As the morning light crept into the gully, Rabbit Fur noticed with fresh eyes the marks of beaver teeth on stumps nearby and the beaver lodge visible in the pond beyond. Her heart jumped. Perhaps the beaver really had visited in the night.

The light of day gave her hope and she dragged herself up to the rock face where the lake was visible. A canoe was coming closer! Rabbit Fur recognized her uncle out searching and calling for her.

"Here I am," she called. "Uncle, Uncle, here I am."

Finally she was safe back at her own wigwam. Rabbit Fur told the story of her dream and the vision of the beaver. Rabbit Fur's people believed that dreams told important messages. Exclaiming happily at the tale, Grandmother cooed and fussed. The ankle would heal, and now, Grandmother was sure that Rabbit Fur would be safe under the protection of a guardian beaver spirit.

The People

The silence and stealth of the woodland hunter, stalking prey or making war, has always been both admired and feared by the white man. The woodland natives could appear suddenly from behind trees and just as quickly melt invisibly into the forest again. They were expert tracers, able to decipher any disturbance on the forest floor such as snapped twigs or over-turned pebbles. They understood many things from animal tracks and droppings, such as the size of the animal, how fast it was going, or the length of time since it had passed by.

These people lived in the southern reaches of the Canadian Shield region–a land of rock, pine, lakes, and muskeg. Large birch trees were plentiful, providing white pliable bark for canoes, wigwams, and containers. The land was more suitable for hunting and trapping than for farming.

Although small plots were made into gardens, most of the food came from the animals of the land. The people had to live as *nomads*, moving from place to place to follow their food source.

Nomads: *people without a permanent dwelling, who wander seasonally following their food source.*

Highly educated about the ways of life in the bush, these people knew when certain fish spawned, what animals were good to eat, and what herbs would cure various illnesses. It required great skill to provide all the necessities of life, and the people helped each other.

Each tribe consisted of numerous bands. A *band* was a small group of related families that lived and hunted together.

Festivities of summer were welcomed when the food was plentiful enough for large gatherings of families. With the coming of winter, the large camp broke up and bands went off to hunt again in small groups, often of just one or two families.

Algonquian *is the language spoken by hunting tribes of the Eastern Woodlands.*
Algonkians *is the name for all these tribes together.*
The ***Algonquin*** *are one tribe in the group of Algonkians.*

Life in an Anishinabe Camp, pp. 4-5; Kids Book of Aboriginal Peoples, pp. 42-43.

Project Book

Make a title page for the Eastern Woodland Hunters.

Food

The Hunters of the Eastern Woodlands had to live closely in tune with the land and the seasons in order to secure what they needed to live. Hunger was a constant threat. They stocked up in times of plenty, so that they could be ready for the lean months.

Moose, bear, deer, and small mammals were both hunted and trapped. The natives used all the parts of the animal, wasting nothing. They were expert fishermen who knew where and when fish were plentiful.

The Ojibway harvested wild rice and all Algonkians gathered berries, nuts, and roots in birch bark baskets. Maple forests provided them with maple sap for syrup and sugar.

The versatile bark of birch trees could be made into useful cooking pots. Baskets were folded, sewn, and then smeared with tree gum to waterproof the seams. A basket filled with water would not burn if the part directly over the flame had water on the other side. Food was cooked by dropping hot rocks into a basket of water using tongs made of green sapling. When cool, the rocks were lifted out and new hot ones put in. This was continued until the water boiled.

Madeline Theriault, a woman born in 1908, learned the ways of the bush from her great-grandparents who raised her. At fifteen years of age she married. Her knowledge of the old ways became very useful while she and her husband lived off the land. Here is an excerpt from one of her stories. What products of nature did she use instead of those purchased from a store?

> . . .we came across a black bear swimming across the lake. We ran him close to shore and my husband shot him. We pulled him out of the water, skinned him and cut off the fat. I cooked it down to make the oil.
> My husband asked, "How are we going to keep this oil? We have no containers."
> Anyway, I went to work and cleaned yards and yards of bear's intestines. I turned them inside out and washed them well in the lake. Next I poured the oil into this bear's intestines. Now I had yards and yards of this bear oil. It is very good for . . . fish frying or moose steak. . . .To keep the oil I made a big birch bark basket and coiled this intestine from the bottom of the basket around and around until filled to the top. When we needed the oil, we just poured it out . . . and tied it back up again. We had enough fat for winter.
> Every year in the fall, all trappers kill a bear for that purpose, to have oil for the winter.[1]

[1] Madeline Katt Theriault, *Moose to Moccasins*. (Toronto: Natural Heritage/Natural History Inc., 1992), pp. 47-48.

Life in an Anishinabe Camp, pp. 22-23; Kids Book of Aboriginal Peoples, p. 46.

Project Book
Colour the correct project picture of the food of this cultural group. Draw additional pictures and/or write things you learned about the food and the gathering of it. Glue notes and pictures in your project book.

Shelter

The houses of the Algonkians could be put up and taken down quickly. This was necessary with their nomadic way of life. The *wigwams* were cone or dome-shaped. The dome-shaped shelter was made by bending green saplings into half-circles, and planting both ends in the ground for the frame. The frame of the conical wigwam was made from long straight poles, either green or dry, tied together at the top. Birch bark, skins, or woven mats were laid over either frame. Another set of poles against the outside held the covering in place.

Inside the shelter, a layer of spruce boughs made sweet-smelling insulation for the floor. The boughs were covered with woven mats or skins. The fire in the centre of the wigwam was necessary for cooking and warmth. Although most of the smoke escaped through a hole in the roof, some of it circulated around the wigwam, which helped to keep the pesky bugs away. The family often slept with their feet facing in towards the fire. This position gave them both warm feet, and the clearest air for breathing.

Wigwams could be put up on any type of ground in the summer or winter. In the winter, the edges were banked with snow to provide insulation. If a hunter killed a large animal several kilometers from camp, it was easier to move the camp to the site of the carcass than to bring all the meat to the camp. When the family moved, they left the poles behind; there were plenty of trees in the next location.

Life in an Anishinabe Camp, pp. 8-12; Kids Book of Aboriginal Peoples, p. 45.

Project Book
Colour the correct project picture of the housing of this cultural group. On lined paper write different things you learned about their shelters. Glue the notes and the picture in your project book.

Moving and Hunting

The land of the eastern woodlands was crisscrossed with numerous lakes and rivers, therefore, travel by canoe was the best method in the mild months. With great skill Algonkians made light birchbark canoes wich were easy to *portage* and easy to repair.

> ***Portage***: *When boats and supplies are carried over a portion of land separating two bodies of water, or around rapids too difficult to navigate*

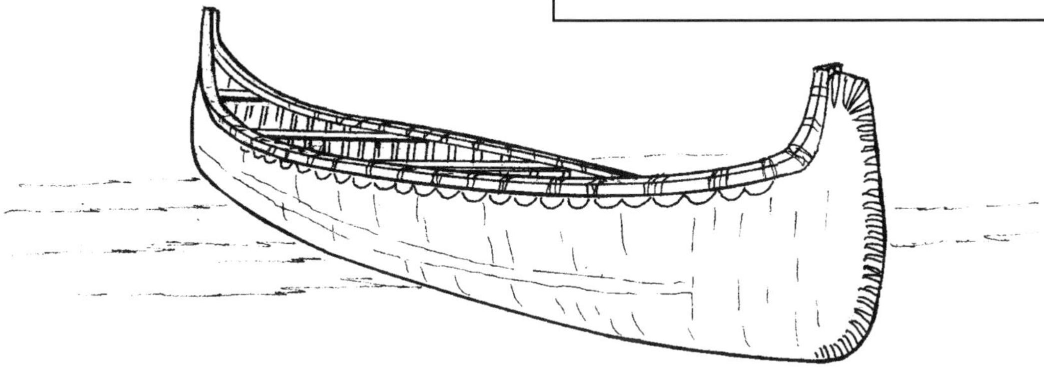

After the winter freeze set in, people used toboggans and snowshoes. When a family moved to a new campsite, the men carried only their weapons for quick use if animals were sighted. Women and children towed their belongings on toboggans. On their mothers' backs, babies were nestled inside cradleboards lined with soft, dried moss or cattail fluff.

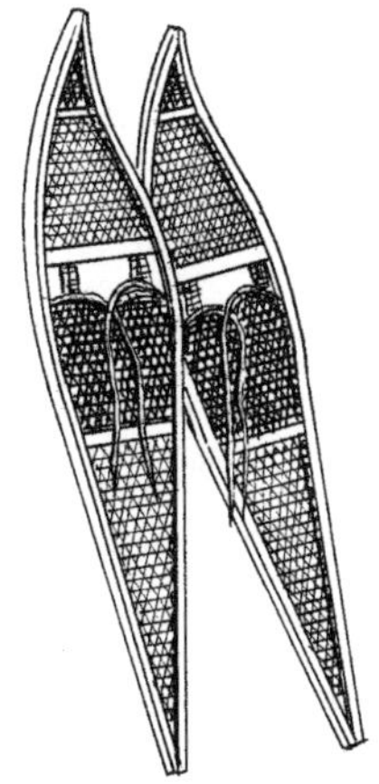

These long, narrow snowshoes were used on hard, packed snow. Round snowshoes were worn when the snowfall was light

While the women set up the wigwams, the men prepared *snares,* which are noose-type traps for small animals. Large animals were hunted by groups of men and dogs because it took many arrows to kill a beast. After the acquisition of guns from the Europeans, hunting became much easier.

Fish were caught in the many rivers and lakes with the help of spears and nets. The Micmac, living near the Atlantic Ocean, used fences called *weirs* which enclosed the fish and left them high in the mud to be gathered easily when the tide went out.

Life in an Anishinabe Camp, pp. 20-21; Kids Book of Aboriginal Peoples, p. 44.

Project Book
Colour the correct project picture of the method of transportation of this cultural group. Add some notes and glue the notes, project picture and any additional material or pictures in your project book.

Work and Customs

The men hunted, while the women tended to the affairs of the campsite. When a kill was made, the women came to help with the butchering and preserving of the food. Women tanned the hides and made moccasins and clothing.

Men would travel to other tribes, especially to the farmers of the south, where furs and canoes were traded for corn or other goods.

In times of fun, the men wrestled, boys raced and girls played "shinny," a form of field hockey. Lacrosse and high jumping were popular. Pick-up-sticks was a quiet game which has been passed on to Canadian children today. Stories and legends were not only enjoyable, but helped to pass tribal beliefs on to the young people.

With their nomadic way of life, Algonkians never believed that land could be owned. It was shared by all, like air and water, since it provided what people needed to live. When the Europeans came, the Algonkians gladly shared their knowledge and resources. They served as guides for the fur traders and explorers.

The Algonkians' furs were prized more highly than those of the Iroquoians, for the animals in a wintry climate develop fuller coats of fur than those of their southern neighbours.

Fierce competition heightened the rivalry among the tribes during the days of the fur trade. Prior to this, there was not much time for war, because securing food and clothing was a constant occupation.

Tanning a Moose Hide

First, the hide was scraped and cleaned, and all the hair cut away. Then a mixture of animal brains and water was spread over the skin and left to soak, softening it. Following this, it was soaked in a water solution for three to four days. Then the hard work of stretching the hide began. It took a whole day to dry, and was stretched back and forth while drying. If it was still hard in places, the process had to be repeated until the skin became soft. Finally, it was smoked over a fire of rotten wood (decaying wood produces much smoke) for several hours on each side. Now it was ready to be made into moccasins, dresses or leggings.

Life in an Anishinabe Camp, pp. 14-17, 24-27; Kids Book of Aboriginal Peoples, p. 47.

Project Book

Using a copy of the map from page 4, colour the correct location of this cultural group. Using a copy of the Eastern Woodland Hunters map, colour the locations of the different tribes of this cultural group. Add the maps to your project book.

Activities

Birchbark basket:

Make a birchbark basket, either from bark you collect from a fallen tree, or of paper. Bark, soaked for several days, will become pliable. The natives always turned the white side in.

The easiest basket to make is the one used to collect maple sap or berries. Four corners of a rectangular piece of bark are folded in and thus there are no seams. Corners can be laced, or just held with two split sticks as shown in the picture.

Another type of basket can be made in various sizes using the pattern shown. The bark was usually sewn with spruce tree roots, but you can use any heavy thread or leather thong. Mark, and then puncture sewing holes with a small nail or tack. Sew a small green branch around the top for the rim.

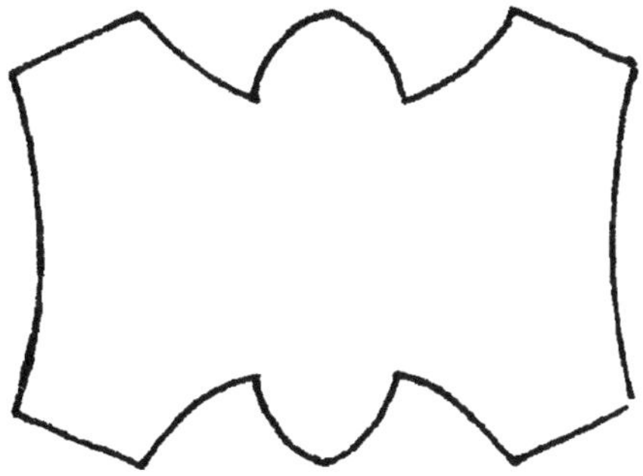

Bowl toss:

Materials needed:	Six clean peach pits
	flat wooden bowl
	beans for counters

Score:	Points
• Six of the same, blanks or spots	10
• Five of the same	5
• Four of the same	3
• Three of the same	1

Method:

1. Paint a black dot on one side of each pit
2. Put pits in the bowl and make teams of 1-3 players.
3. First player shakes bowl and bangs it down hard on the floor
4. Score the pits how they land in the bowl and use a bean for each point.

Vocabulary

nomadic	*wigwam*	*snare*
band	*portage*	*weir*

Eastern Woodland Hunters Workpage

In the right order number the following steps of tanning a moose hide.

______ Stretch and dry the hide.

______ Scrape off all the hair.

______ Spread brains over skin to soak.

______ Cut and sew clothing.

______ Hang hide over smoky fire.

______ Soak in water three to four days.

Complete this page and add it to your project book.

Natives of the Subarctic

Recommended Resources

Available in most libraries

Cass, James. *Ochechak the Caribou Hunter, Indians of the Subarctic.* Toronto: Heath Canada Ltd. and Royal Ontario Museum, 1983. Good information and colour drawings (All grades).

Humber, Charles J. gen. ed., *Canada's Native Peoples.* Mississauga: Heirloom Pub. Inc., 1988. Indians of the N.W.T., Yukon and British Columbia Interior after the European influence (Upper grades).

Irwin, R. Stephen. *Hunters of the Northern Forest.* Surrey: Hancock House Pub. Ltd., 1984. Focusing on the hunting methods of Natives of the Subarctic (Upper grades).

Kalman, Bobbie. *Life in an Anishinabe Camp*. St. Catharines: Crabtree Press, 2003. Native Nations of North America Series (All grades).

Kalman, Bobbie. *Native Homes*. St. Catharines: Crabtree Press, 2001. Native Nations of NA (All grades).

Karp, Barry. *The Cree of James Bay.* Scarborough: Nelson Canada. 1985. Stories remembered by a grandmother, of the life of a Cree family long ago (All grades).

Macfie, John and Johnston, Basil. *Hudson Bay Watershed, A Photographic Memoir of the Ojibway, Cree, and Oji-Cree*. Toronto: Dundurn Press. 1991.

National Film Board of Canada. *Cree Hunters of Mistassini.* 1989. Three Cree families live off their land east of James Bay (Video, All grades).

Ridington, Robin & Jillian. *People of the Trail*. Vancouver: Douglas & McIntyre Ltd., 1978. Good for further information with black and white illustrations (Middle grades).

Silvey, Diane. *The Kids Book of Aboriginal Peoples.* Toronto: Kids Can Press, 2005. Great information and full colour paintings. An all inclusive Canadian book (All grades).

Starvation Winter

A true story by Jacob Kitchacappo of James Bay
Translated by Lillian Small

I can remember my grandmother really (well) but not my grandfather. I remember she lived with us and it was she and my father who taught me how to hunt and trap. I remember, when I was growing up, this one year there were three families living at our camp. Everything was very scarce that year; it was so hard to get any kind of game that we almost starved. We were all losing weight and getting weak and yet every day I would go out and try to find some food for the family to eat. Sometimes, I wouldn't eat for three or four days and when I did have something to eat, I'd eat very little, like one small ptarmigan wing or something like that. At last the older folks couldn't go outdoors, as they were too weak from not eating for so many days.

One day, I was alone walking in the bush, when I came to some moose tracks. I thought, "I have to follow those moose tracks. I might catch up to them." But I couldn't go very fast; so, that evening I had to turn back, because I had to check on the family at the camp. They were all still alive when I got back.

I got up very early the next morning and left the camp. I knew I would have to try very hard this time to catch up with those moose, as we needed the meat very badly. I was feeling kind of weak but I still kept on going.

At last I caught up with them and saw that there (were) two of them. I shot and killed them both. I was so happy! If I hadn't killed those moose I believe that I wouldn't be living today. All three families at our camp would have starved to death that year.

I remember another time when I was younger; we were trapping some two hundred miles up the Eastmain River. It was a very bad year again. Everything was very scarce. One of the men at the camp starved to death. I remember we had to eat the moose hide from an old pair of snowshoes. That's how hungry we were!

Once in awhile I still get hungry, because I haven't very much money to buy what I'd like to eat or what my family needs.[1]

Note: The illustration shows the hunter using a bow as did natives of long ago. The man in this story would have hunted with a gun.

[1] Lillian Small, comp., *Indian Stories from James Bay.* (Cobalt, ON: Highway Book Shop, 1972) p. 6.

The People

The haunting wildness of Canada's north woods stirs up images of howling wolves and voyageurs. It has been said that "once a person has been to the boreal forest, he will never forget it." The boreal forest includes shimmering white-barked birch trees along with pine, spruce, and fast growing poplars. North of the boreal forest, the trees thin out until finally the land is bare and the tundra stretches like a sea, bleak and desolate.

The Natives of the Subarctic dwelt in one of the most difficult environments for survival. The hardships were tremendous. Long cold winters made travelling and hunting difficult. The warmth of the summers brought the tormenting swarms of blood-sucking mosquitoes and black flies. The land, however, provided all that the natives needed to survive.

The Natives of the Subarctic are divided into two main language families. The eastern tribes spoke various forms of Algonquian. The Chipewyan, Beaver, and all tribes northwest of them spoke Athapaskan. These Athapaskans now refer to themselves as the Dene people.

*The **boreal forest** is a vast band of coniferous (evergreen) trees south of the treeless tundra.*

*The **tundra** is land in a northern area where the ground is frozen so much of the year that trees cannot grow. The land is covered with grass, lichen and moss.*

A woman hauls a load using a **tumpline**—a band across her forehead. The women of the Subarctic were the burden bearers

Project Book
Make a title page for the Natives of the Subarctic.

Food

No animal was more important to subarctic existence than the herds of caribou which roamed the land. With thousands in a herd, they could very shortly over-graze the fragile tundra and therefore, they were always on the move. Winter found them foraging for food in the shelter of the boreal forest. Each spring, they made an annual migration to graze on 'caribou moss' on the tundra.

They followed familiar patterns of migration, crossing rivers and streams at the same point each year. By the time caribou calves were a few hours old, they could follow their mothers in a crossland trek.

It was the reliability of these annual migrations that lent security to the existence of the Natives of the Subarctic. The hunt during the fall migration was the most important of the year, in order to provide food and skins for the long winter ahead. If the herd changed its migration pattern and the natives failed in the hunt, great hardship, or possible starvation would follow. Food, clothing, tents, rope, and tools all came from the caribou.

The Natives of the Subarctic also relied on bear, moose, and small mammals, such as beaver and rabbit. Spring was a happy time when the ice broke up and the rivers teemed with fish. Children called the parents at the sounds of returning ducks and geese which were then lured into arrow range with decoys

and bird calls.

The northern lands are the summer breeding grounds for many ducks and geese, thus providing a wide variety of eggs to be gathered. Blueberries, cranberries, saskatoon berries and currants were also picked in the short growing season.

Kids Book of Aboriginal Peoples, pp. 32-33.

Project Book
Colour the correct project picture of the food of this cultural group. Draw additional pictures and/ or write things you learned about the food and the gathering of it. Glue notes and pictures in your project book.

Shelter

The Natives of the Subarctic were *nomadic;* they were always on the move in search of food. Do you think they made wigwams like the Algonkian hunters, or longhouses like the Iroquoian farmers? Why?

If you said, "Like the Algonkian hunters," you were right. These people could not build permanent homes because they were moving often. Poles tied in a cone shape were covered with bark or caribou skins. If bark was not available, caribou skins were sewn together to make a tent, similar to the tipi of the plains. The only difference was that there were no flaps at the top of the subarctic wigwam to release smoke like the tipi. From early spring, right through to the end of summer, clouds of mosquitoes and black flies pestered any warm-blooded creature; thus, the smoke was allowed to circulate constantly through the wigwam to keep the bugs away.

David Thompson, the great explorer and mapmaker of the 1700's, comments on the good qualities of birch bark for shelters.

> For coverings to their tents and lodges, Rind (birch bark) is sewed together so as to take the form required; and being water proof, make a light comfortable tent in all weathers, and when the rain is over, the natives can directly remove; whereas a leather tent when soaked with rain, requires a day's time and fire to dry it. Unfortunately the cold of winter renders it brittle and liable to accidents; and it must be warmed before it can be rolled up for removal; and the same to unroll it.[1]

[1] Thompson, *Narrative.* p. 116.

Native Homes, pp. 12-13. *Kids Book of Aboriginal Peoples*, pp. 30-31.

Project Book
Colour the correct project picture of the housing of this cultural group. On lined paper write different things you learned about their shelters. Glue the notes and the picture in your project book.

Moving and Hunting

Being *nomadic*, Natives of the Subarctic were always on the move in search of food. Wherever there were rivers, they travelled in bark canoes. Much of the land, however, had to be crossed on foot. Travel was difficult over rough land that included bogs, incessant blackflies in spring, or snowbound forests in winter.

In the summer, loads were carried in packs held by *tumplines,* bands that went across the forehead. In the winter, snowshoes and toboggans made travel easier.

Like the Algonkian natives, the men would travel ready to shoot game, while women and children carried all of the belongings. Possessions would be stored in a pit or platform *cache* until the season in which it was needed again.

Successful hunters had to intimately know the ways of their quarry. Stealth and silence marked their skill. A startled moose could trot far out of range in a short time. The struggle for food was too serious to risk failure.

In the picture, the hunter sees moose tracks, and stays downwind of them. Since moose often travel in circles, the hunter moves a distance away from the tracks. He goes up to the tracks to check that he is on the right course. Eventually, he sights the moose without startling it by his scent.

Caribou, following the same yearly migration patterns, had favourite river crossings in their fall passage from the tundra. Native hunters would gather in canoes to ambush the animals in the water where the kill was easier. The foreleg of a dead animal was hooked over the antlers (both male and female have antlers). This method kept the nose and mouth above water and the animal floated until gathered after the hunt.

Groups of hunters sometimes drove the caribou through a funnel-shaped passage leading into a fenced pen, where the animals were killed with arrows. This was a dangerous job and many men worked together. In the boreal forest in the winter, caribou were disadvantaged by deep snow. A lone hunter on snowshoes could usually track and overtake a foraging animal.

Kids Book of Aboriginal Peoples, pp. 34-35.

Project Book
Colour the correct project picture of the method of transportation of this cultural group. Add some notes and glue the notes, project picture and any additional material or pictures in your project book.

Work and Customs

The Natives of the Subarctic were spread far apart across the vast expanse of land. Hunters often set out trap lines that covered a great distance. Under the threat of storms and wolves, they had to pay close attention to their surroundings to avoid getting lost, as there would be no one to come to the rescue in case of mishap.

Warmer seasons brought large groups together, while in the winter, the families separated into small bands of two or three families.

Since a set of warm winter clothing required up to seven caribou skins, the women were constantly busy tanning hides, or sewing and mending clothing for their family. Women were also the burden bearers, carrying and packing meat from their husbands' kill.

David Thompson became intimately acquainted with the ways of the Natives of the Subarctic. He admired their kind manners and generosity with each other. He writes the following words:

After reading, discuss with your teacher what the second paragraph of the quote means. Is David Thompson praising the civilized society, or the so-called 'Savages'?

> The natives in their manners are mild and decent, treat each other with kindness and respect, and very rarely interrupt each other in conversation;
>
> ....those acts that pass between man and man for generous charity and kind compassion in civilized society (Europeans) are no more than what is every day practised by these Savages; as acts of common duty; is any one unsuccessful in the chase, has he lost his little all by some accident, he is sure to be relieved by the others to the utmost of their power.[1]

[1] Ibid., p. 81.

Life in a Plains Camp, pp. 4-17

Project Book

Using a copy of the map from page 4, colour the correct location of this cultural group. Using a copy of the Natives of the Subarctic map, colour the locations of the different tribes of this cultural group. Add the maps to your project book.

Thanadelthur
Slave Woman

Exclaiming in surprise, the trader bent over the still figure covered in snow. No sign of life! The deerskin clothing was torn, barely covering the gaunt figure. Shaking his head the trader stood up. He knew the dangers of this wild land. The line between life and death was very thin.

Suddenly his ears perked up. The trader leaned forward. Was that a groan? He nudged the prone woman with his snowshoe and she rolled back and groaned again. Alive! She needed shelter quickly. Carrying her to a grove of trees, he laid her down gently and coaxed a fire to life. Soon, a pot of snow was melting to provide water to make a nourishing cup of hot tea.

The woman revived and was carried back to York Factory, a trading post on Hudson Bay. She told her story about being captured by the Cree and finally escaping, only to become lost and starving in the northern wilderness.

The fur traders wanted to open up trade with her people, the Chipewyans. Cree warriors, with guns, had kept the Chipewyans from the trading posts. The Chipewyans did not have the advantage of firearms.

Thanadelthur, known to the traders only as Slave Woman, regained her health and became recognized for her strength of character. She was asked to head up a peace mission to her people.

In June, 1715, she set out with 148 Crees and a British trader, William Stuart. They travelled for days over the barrens in search of Thanadelthur's Chipewyan relatives. Once they couldn't find food for over eight days. Storms and hunger made many want to turn back, but she urged them on.

They came to a tragic battle scene where many Chipewyans lay frozen in the snow, killed by the gunshots of Crees. The troop refused to travel farther. They were afraid the Chipewyans would blame them for the deaths.

Thanadelthur persuaded them to wait there for her, for ten days, and she set out alone to find the Chipewyans. At last she reached their camp where warriors had gathered to plan revenge for the death of their friends. They looked on her with suspicion, but agreed to hear her plea.

For three days, Thanadelthur talked and argued with her people. She gave them gifts from the British and described the things their furs could buy. Finally, exhausted, she succeeded in persuading them to come back with her and seek peace with the Cree.

On exactly the tenth day, just as Stuart and the Crees were preparing to head back, Thanadelthur came stumbling in with 160 of her people. Her efforts brought peace to the Chipewyans and opened up much of the north and west to the fur trade.

Activities

Tumpline:
Make a tumpline from a piece of cloth or an old belt. Try carrying a loaded pack using the tumpline over your forehead. If you like, decorate it with fur or beads.
With which do you think heavier loads can be carried, shoulder straps, or forehead straps?

Snowshoes:
Different shapes of snowshoes were used for different types of snow. Try to find out some information about snowshoes. If you have access to snowshoes, try them out.

Vocabulary

boreal forest	*tumpline*
tundra	*downwind*

Natives of the Subarctic

Write the name of each picture in the spaces below. Then, write the boxed letter from each word on the *mystery animal* line, to find the cute, furry animal whose Native name has become an English word.

1. ☐ _ _ _ _

2. _ _ _ _ _ _ ☐ _ _ _

3. _ ☐ _ _ _ _

4. _ _ _ ☐ _ _ _ _

5. ☐ _ _ _ _

6. _ _ _ _ _ _ _ ☐

7. _ _ _ _ _ _ _ _ ☐

8 _ _ _ _ _ _ _ _ _ ☐

Mystery Animal: _ _ _ _ _ _ _ _ _

Complete this page and add it to your project book.

Natives of the Plains

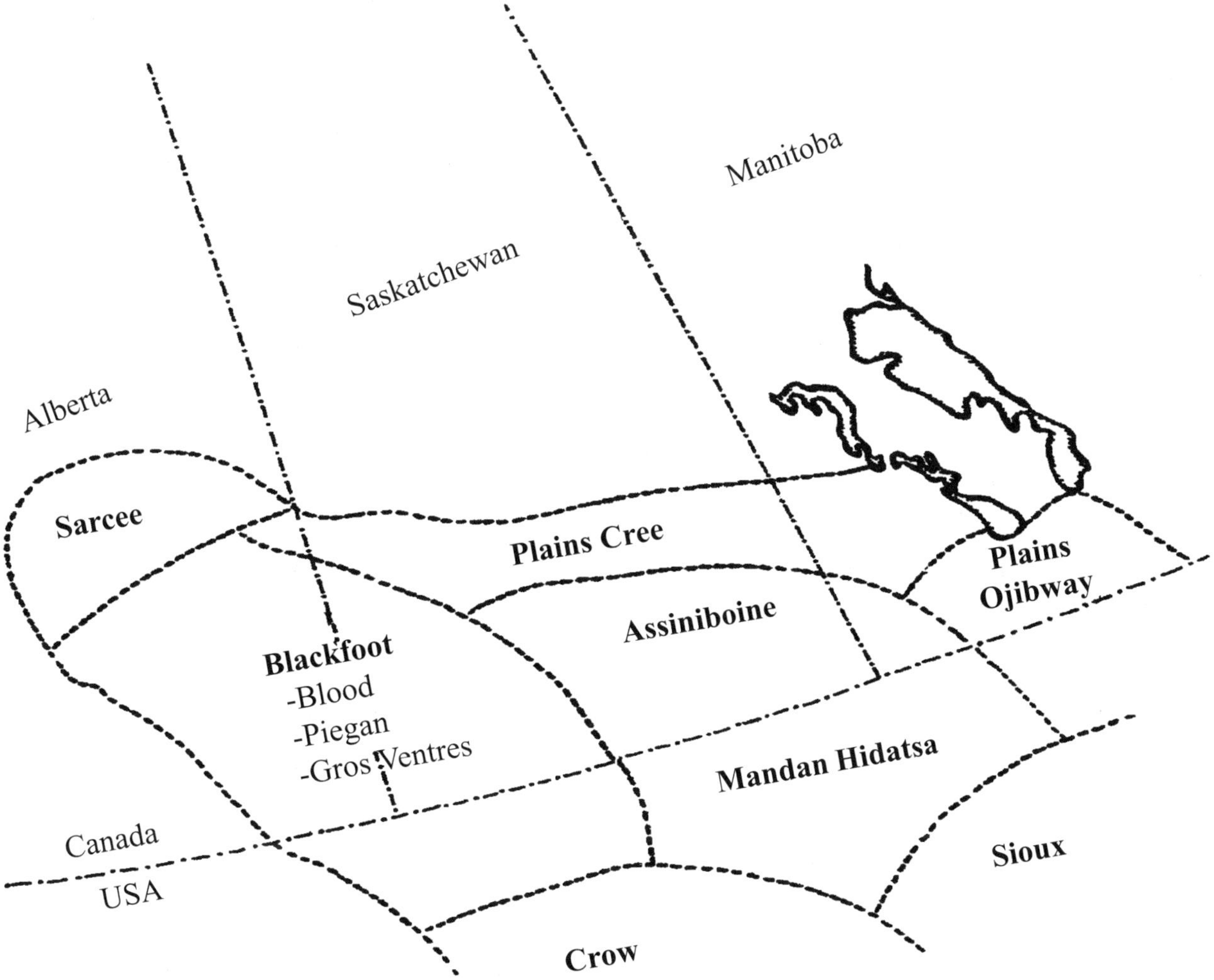

Recommended Resources

Available in most libraries

Brass, Eleanor. *I Walk in Two Worlds*. Calgary: Glenbow-Alberta Institute. 1987. Informative life story of a Saskatchewan woman born in 1905. (Upper grades)

Bruchac, Joseph. *A Boy Called Slow.* New York: Philomel Books, 1994. A picture book of the true story of how Sitting Bull got his name. (Early grades)

Barnett, Donald C. *Poundmaker.* Don Mills: Fitzhenry & Whiteside Ltd., 1976. Plains Cree chief charged in the NorthWest Rebellion of 1885 (Middle & upper grades).

Cass, James. *Mistatin, the Buffalo Hunter*. Toronto: Heath Canada Ltd. and the Royal Ontario Museum, 1983. Good information with colour pictures. (All grades)

Dion, Joseph F. *My Tribe the Crees*. Calgary: Glenbow-Alberta Institute, 1979. As a descendent of Big Bear, Dion relates the history of his people from a Native viewpoint (Upper grades).

Holling, C. Holling. *The Book of Indians.* New York: Platt & Munk Co., 1962, Chapters 5-7. In true Holling style, delightful fictional stories designed to teach (All grades).

Kalman, Bobbie. *Life in an Plains Camp*. St. Catharines: Crabtree Press, 2003. Native Nations of North America Series well worth having on your bookshelf (All grades).

Kalman, Bobbie. *Native Homes*. St. Catharines: Crabtree Press, 2001. Native Nations of NA (All grades).

Luling, Virginia. *Indians of the North American Plains.* England: Macdonald Educational, 1978. An excellent information book with full-colour pictures (All grades).

Neihardt, John. *Black Elk Speaks.* New York: William Morrow & Co., 1932. Black Elk was a Lacota Plains Indian during the last days of the buffalo. An American story, but gives insight on all Plains Natives. Chapters need not be read consecutively. We especially enjoyed the tape by Audio Literature, 1991 (All grades).

Schultz, James Willard. *Blackfeet and Buffalo, Memories of Life Among the Indians.* Norman: University of Oklahoma Press, 1962 Captivating stories by a man who married into and lived with the Blackfeet, 1878-1915. Pick and choose chapters (Upper grades).

Schultz, James Willard. *My Life As An Indian.* Forest and Stream Pub. Co., 1907. New York: Fawcett Columbine Books, CBS Publications, 1981 (Upper grades).

Silvey, Diane. *The Kids Book of Aboriginal Peoples.* Toronto: Kids Can Press, 2005. Great information and full colour paintings. An all inclusive Canadian book (All grades).

Stuart, Gene S. *Three Little Indians.* National Geographic Society, 1974. Short story of a Cheyenne boy from a U.S. tribe, but very typical of Canadian Plains Natives (Early to middle grades).

Swan-Jackson, Alys. *The Plains Indians.* (See-Through History Series) Great Britain: Reed International Books Ltd., 1995. Full-colour pictures and easy text (All grades).

Thom, Laine. *Becoming Brave, The Path to Native American Manhood.* San Francisco: Chronicle Books, 1992. Excellent first person stories and pictures of the making of an Indian brave (Middle to upper grades).

Buffalo Hunt

We boys fairly danced with excitement as we jumped up on our ponies and pulled in behind the throng of people moving out. We yearned to race like the wind past each slow woman's horse with a travois, but we dared not. Only hunting advisors rode in front, followed by the chiefs, for we were on our way for the big buffalo hunt!

When the sun was high, we camped. While the women were cooking, the shout came, "The scouts are coming back!" Three men on horseback came over the hill. All the people thronged to the centre of the village as the scouts rode up to the council tipi. The other boys and I scrambled to see, and I ducked to look between the legs of a tall hunter.

The scouts sat at the door of the council tipi while an advisor lit the sacred pipe. Each scout smoked the pipe, to prove that his words would be true.

"Now!" said the advisor. "Tell what you have seen."

They spoke slowly in turn. They told first of a small buffalo herd, then a larger one, and then, beyond a hill, buffalo as far as the eye could see!

So, the hunt was on! Excitement filled the air as everyone readied ponies and weapons for the great gathering of meat.

Then we all started out towards the bison. First, were the soldiers, riding twenty abreast (one-beside the other). No one dared disobey their rules or he might get knocked off his horse.

After the soldiers rode the hunters, coming five abreast. The rest of us came in behind. The hunters carefully circled around the buffalo. Then they all shouted, "Hoka hey!" and everyone charged in to kill.

We boys, on our ponies, watched and yelled in the dust and noise, but no one noticed us.

By nightfall, the butchering was done. The women hung all the meat in strips on racks to dry. We played a war game with those strips of meat. Our teacher would take us away from the village. We would pretend that it was an enemy village and we were coming to steal horses.

We crawled in the grass towards the tipis, then snuck in and snatched strips of meat. If we came back without getting caught, we had a feast, a dance and told our brave stories. Once I had no brave story to tell. I had been in a tree, reaching for meat when a man came from his tipi and yelled "Ye-a-a!" I was so scared, that I fell out of the tree and ran away crying. The man had only been yelling at his dog!

Those days of the buffalo hunt, they were happy times.

Based on a true story.[1]

[1] John Neihardt. *Black Elk Speaks.* (New York: William Morrow & Co., 1932).

The People

The buffalo on the prairies were an immense force to be reckoned with, unpredictable and easily stampeded. Prior to the acquisition of horses, prairie nomads had a difficult life trying to keep up with roaming herds of buffalo. Acquiring horses, and later, guns, elevated the Natives of the Plains to their most glorious days. With the dwindling of the buffalo and the coming of white settlement, the traditional way of life was destroyed.

The **horse travois**, two poles tied to the horse, which dragged on the ground, helped carry heavy loads when moving from one camp to another.

By the time writers showed serious interest in recording the lifestyles of the natives of North America, the eastern tribes had already been displaced or their traditional ways drastically altered. European adventurers became enchanted with the vast untamed plains and the people who still roamed after the buffalo. Painters, traders, and storytellers recorded for the world what had previously been handed down only by oral history.

Thus, there is a vast array of material documenting the life of the Natives of the Plains. It was the plains warrior that wore the eagle feather headdress and became a well-known figure in cowboy and Indian stories. It is fun to imagine galloping across the plains on horseback, free as the wind, but the true picture is not as romantic.

These people worked hard to survive, roaming the vast grasslands we call the prairies. The prairies stretch from the centre of Canada, down to the central United States. There were no country borders long ago. The tribes followed the buffalo wherever the herds went because they provided all the natives needed.

Clothing, moccasins, tipis and saddles were all made from buffalo hides. Bones and sinews were used to make tools and weapons. Most importantly, buffalo were the main source of food for the Natives of the Plains.

Life in a Plains Camp, pp. 4-5, 8-11; *Kids Book of Aboriginal Peoples*, p. 18.

Project Book
Make a title page for the Natives of the Plains.

Food

People of the plains hunted other mammals such as moose, deer and rabbit; but buffalo was the most readily available and the preferred meat. Some of the meat from a hunt was cooked immediately, however much of it was cut into thin strips and dried on racks in the sun. Dried meat was called *jerky*. Jerky could be pounded into powder and mixed with melted animal fat and berries to make *pemmican*.

Pemmican lasted years without spoiling and provided a high energy staple. It was carried by warriors in a leather pouch called a *parflech* (pronounced "parflesh")

Pemmican was a major food source on the trail and throughout the long winters. It became an important commodity for fur traders and explorers.

Although they were mostly eaters of meat, the Natives of the Plains also gathered edible wild plants and berries in season.

Modern tastes will not readily appreciate the taste of pemmican. It should be remembered that when you're hungry on the trail, anything tastes good. The high fat content of pemmican was necessary for the health of natives who expended a great amount of physical energy in everyday life.

Native women varied their recipe with different amounts and types of dried fruit. Just as any cook today loves to impress friends with the best recipe, so a native woman would be proud to make the best pemmican.

Today, pemmican can be made using dried beef.

Use a food blender or processor to grind dried beef to powder. For each 500 grams, add 125 ml of raisins. Put in a shallow pan and pour just enough hot fat from bacon or other meat over it to hold the beef and raisins together. Mix thoroughly and cool. Cut into squares or strips. Pemmican can be stored for some time.[1]

[1] Marz and Nono Minor. *The American Indian Craft Book.* (Lincoln:University of Nebraska Press, 1972), p. 115.

Life in a Plains Camp, pp. 14-17; *Kids Book of Aboriginal Peoples*, p. 19.

Project Book

Colour the correct project picture of the food of this cultural group. Draw additional pictures and/or write things you learned about the food and the gathering of it. Glue notes and pictures in your project book.

Shelter

> The sun and the sky, the earth and the moon are round like a shield,. . . . The day, the night, and the moon go in a circle above the sky. . . .
>
> For these reasons the (Oglala) make their tipis circular, their camp circle circular, and sit in a circle in all ceremonies. The circle is also the symbol of the tipi and of shelters.[1]

The shelters of the plains people were *tipis*, large cone-shaped frames covered by buffalo hides. A tipi could be set up in a very short time by several people. Many hides were needed and each year fresh ones were tanned and sewn to create new white covers. Flaps at the top were opened to release smoke when a fire was needed inside for warmth or cooking. The flaps could be adjusted according to the direction of the wind.

Inside, furs spread on the ground insulated the floor and provided bedding. A fire of dried buffalo dung burned in the centre of the tipi. Inner liners were hung to the floor from halfway up to prevent draughts. Food and belongings dangled in a leather pouch or parfleche. Family members reclined against willow-branch back rests hung from small tripods. The most important person sat farthest from the doorway. It was never polite to pass between someone and the fire; so, a person would lean forward to let someone move in or out behind them. Symbolic designs of spirit helpers were painted on the outsides of tipis. Shields and medicine bundles, small bags of sacred objects, were hung from poles behind a tipi. It was thought that these had spiritual powers to protect the dwellers of the tipi from enemies. So strong was the superstition, that enemies, seeing the medicine bundles, would be afraid to come closer for fear that evil would befall them. The tipis in a camp were set up in a semicircle, with all the doors facing the rising sun.

[1] Norman Bancroft-Hunt. *The Indians of the Great Plains.* (New York: Peter Bedrick Books, 1989), pp. 103-4.

Native Homes, pp. 18-20; Life in a Plains Camp, pp. 6-7.

Project Book

Colour the correct project picture of the housing of this cultural group. On lined paper write different things you learned about their shelters. Glue the notes and the picture in your project book.

Moving and Hunting

Horses were not present in North America many years ago. Spaniards first brought them across the Atlantic Ocean to Mexico. They spread northward and by 1700, most plains tribes had trained them for transportation and hunting.

Before the horse, people walked to follow buffalo herds. The men travelled ahead carrying only weapons. In this way they were able to shoot game or protect their families from enemies. The women carried the babies and heavy bundles. Dogs pulled belongings on a *travois* made from tent poles. Travel at such a slow pace made following great buffalo herds difficult.

After the acquisition of horses, transportation became much easier. A horse could carry far more on a *travois* than dogs and greater distances could be covered.

The plains people had various methods for hunting buffalo. Prior to horses, bands would join together and build a large corral, with a long funnel-shaped doorway. Shouting hunters would drive buffalo into the corral and then kill them with spears and arrows.

Another method was to stampede the buffalo over a cliff where they would fall to their deaths. In southern Alberta, layers of buffalo bones have been unearthed at the bottom of a cliff called Head-Smashed-In Buffalo Jump.

With horses, the natives could ride alongside and among the buffalo. Arrows required a close range. Guns became available later, but the expert hunter could be just as successful with arrows. A native Canadian of the Cree tribe tells the following hunting story.

> John Keheewin, or Eagle, was known to have killed four buffalo with one and the same arrow. In cooperation with his well-trained horse, he knew exactly where to place the shaft; then with only the feathered part showing he pulled the arrow out of one buffalo and with it shot another and another; the fourth buffalo fell before he could retrieve his arrow.[1]

Plains people came to depend on horses more and more. Horses became symbols of wealth. Many were needed to transport a family's belongings.

Each hunter had a buffalo pony used strictly in the chase. It was fast and well-trained. These valuable horses were not put to pasture with the others, but were tethered next to the owner's tipi where thieving would be riskier.

Hunts required cooperation. A man who hunted alone was seriously punished, for by carelessness, one man could spook and stampede a herd, bringing about failure for everyone. Native police, called dog soldiers, enforced strict rules.

After the hunt, everyone helped with the butchering. The meat was shared, but the hide was the possession of the man who had killed the animal.

---

[1] Joseph F. Dion. *My Tribe the Crees.* (Calgary: Glenbow Museum, 1979), p. 28.

Life in a Plains Camp, pp. 12-13; Kids Book of Aboriginal Peoples, pp. 20-21.

Project Book
Colour the correct project picture of the method of transportation of this cultural group. Add some notes and glue the notes, project picture and any additional material or pictures in your project book.

Work and Customs

The roles of men and women were clearly defined. The women collected berries, plants, or roots, and then prepared and cooked all the food. They took down tipis when moving camp. Tanning hides for shelter and clothing was fatiguing work shared by all women. A desirable wife was one who had the skills to provide food and clothing for her husband.

Men excelled at hunting and war. Ten-year-old boys were allowed to accompany hunting men. By the teen years, a boy would be well experienced and able to provide food for those in his band.

There were two other qualities that made a man *a man*, in the eyes of friends and elders: bravery and generosity.

Any courageous act, whether noble or foolhardy, counted as a *coup*. A warrior could count coup by such acts as taking an enemy's weapon or horse, or being the first to touch a dead enemy. It was considered a greater coup to touch a live enemy than to kill him.

Warriors who were brave in battle or hunting were awarded a coup feather. A man could not marry without at least one coup. Every eagle feather in the feather headdresses of chiefs had a valiant story behind it.

When horses became available they were the measure of a man's wealth. Stealing horses from an enemy tribe was considered good, for it displayed daring and courage. A father would prefer his son to die in battle, showing bravery, than to live to old age.

> So important was this virtue that when a boy was born, his father held him up to the sun and prayed: "O Sun. Make this boy strong and brave. May he die in battle rather than from old age or sickness."[1]

Generosity was another quality highly valued. The survival of a band depended on the hunter sharing his spoils with the whole group. Only the man highly respected as brave and generous could ever become a chief. Only chiefs and old men had enough coups to wear the full-length feather headdress of the Natives of the Plains.

---

1 John C. Ewers "The Horse in Blackfoot Indian Culture," *Bureau of American Ethnology Bulletin 159*. (Washington: 1955) Cited by Howard L Harrod *Mission Among the Blackfeet* (University of Oklahoma Press., 1971), p. 4.

Life in a Plains Camp, pp. 18-29; Kids Book of Aboriginal Peoples, pp. 22-23.

Project Book
Using a copy of the map from page 4, colour the correct location of this cultural group. Using a copy of the Natives of the Plains map, colour the locations of the different tribes of this cultural group. Add the maps to your project book.

Who's Who?

Western Native Leaders of the Late 1800's

Big Bear (Cree) 1825-1888

Big Bear, the Cree chief, was the first of the prairie chiefs to refuse to sign a treaty with the Canadian government. He refused to give up the free life of the hunt for life on a reserve. All the resistant young braves followed him and he struggled to restrain their violent passion. In 1879, when roaming buffalo disappeared for good, the Cree had lost their means of survival.

Big Bear was forced to sign Treaty No. 6 in 1882. When Cree warriors attacked and killed white people at Frog Lake, Big Bear's attempts at peace fell on deaf ears. He was old. They no longer listened to him. Big Bear's influence prevented the loss of lives in subsequent rebellions, but in the end he was charged and convicted as a participant in the North West Rebellion.

Big Bear served two years in Stoney Mountain Penitentiary in Manitoba. He died shortly after his release in the winter of 1888.

Crowfoot (Blackfoot) 1830-1890

Crowfoot, the leading chief of the Blackfoot confederacy, drew admiration from all for his courage and wisdom. As a young man, he single-handedly killed a grizzly bear that had just mauled a Blackfoot child.

Crowfoot was a peacemaker. He was friendly to missionaries and traders. He made a peace agreement with his longtime enemies, the Cree, and adopted the Cree chief, Poundmaker, as a son. He warmly welcomed the police who brought order to the west.

Crowfoot's decision to sign Treaty No. 7 in 1877 influenced other chiefs to follow. In 1885, he kept the Blackfoot out of the North West Rebellion. Although he mistrusted the government's promises, he knew a fight would not improve his people's plight.

Poundmaker (Cree) 1842-1886

Poundmaker was not a prominent chief until the North West Rebellion. In 1872, when the Cree and Blackfoot tribes settled ancient disagreements, Poundmaker became Crowfoot's adopted son as a guarantee of peace. They enjoyed a strong friendship.

Poundmaker had reluctantly signed Treaty No. 6 with other chiefs in 1876 and settled on his reserve near Battleford, Saskatchewan. He was generally a peacemaker. When the government cut rations to save money, his people were starving. In 1885, they lashed back by looting the town of Battleford. Government troops launched an attack at Cut Knife Hill and were solidly defeated. Poundmaker stopped the natives from pursuing the government soldiers and thus prevented a massacre. Refusing to join forces with Metis uprisings, Poundmaker voluntarily surrendered. He was sentenced to three years in prison. Extremely ill with tuberculosis, he was released within six months, but died in Crowfoot's home a few weeks later.

Sitting Bull (Sioux) 1834-1890
Crazy Horse (Oglala Sioux) 1844-1877

These two American chiefs were leaders in the defeat of Custer's USA forces in 1876. They fled for some time into Canada until they were persuaded to return to the USA reservations. Sitting Bull was killed mistakenly in a volley of gunfire with USA soldiers. Crazy Horse was killed by knife wounds when he resisted USA officers.

Activities

Feather Headdress:

Using turkey feathers available from a butcher, make a feather headdress as found in:

The Complete Book of Indian Crafts and Lore. by W. Ben Hunt
New York: Golden Press, 1954. (1970 - 21st printing)
This is an intensive project for older students.
Related reading: Schultz, "The Making of a Warrior," *Blackfeet and Buffalo,* pp. 144-154.

Younger students might try the Blackfoot headdress found in:

Make It Work: North American Indians. by Andrew Haslam and Alexandra Parsons
Great Britain: Two-Can Pub. Ltd., 1995.

Meat Grabber (a game):

Cut strips of cloth (red) to represent drying meat and hang them along the edge of a table or on a chair. One person, blindfolded, with a rolled up magazine or newspaper in hand, stands in front of the table to guard the "meat" by swinging the newspaper around. Another child has to sneak in and grab as much "meat" as possible without being touched with the newspaper. This game is a lot of fun. Take turns and switch places.

Vocabulary

travois	*pemmican*	*coup*
jerky	*parfleche*	*tipi*

Natives of the Plains Workpage

Down:
1. Part of a bird used to make a warrior's headdress.
2. Leather pouch used for carrying pemmican.
3. Put on a dog or horse for carrying loads.
4. Warriors counted ___?___ for brave acts.
5. Name of a northern plains tribe.
6. The method of acquiring food.

Across:
1. Dried and ground beef mixed with fat and berries.
2. Animal which made life easier for the Natives of the Plains.
3. Most important resource for Natives of the Plains.
4. Head man of a tribe.
5. Doors of tipis always faced the rising _______
___?___ .
6. The home of Natives of the Plains.

Choose from the following words:

buffalo	**eagle**	**parfleche**	**tipi**
chief	**horse**	**pemmican**	**travois**
coup	**hunt**	**sun**	**feather**
Cree			

Complete this page and add it to your project book.

Natives of the Plateau

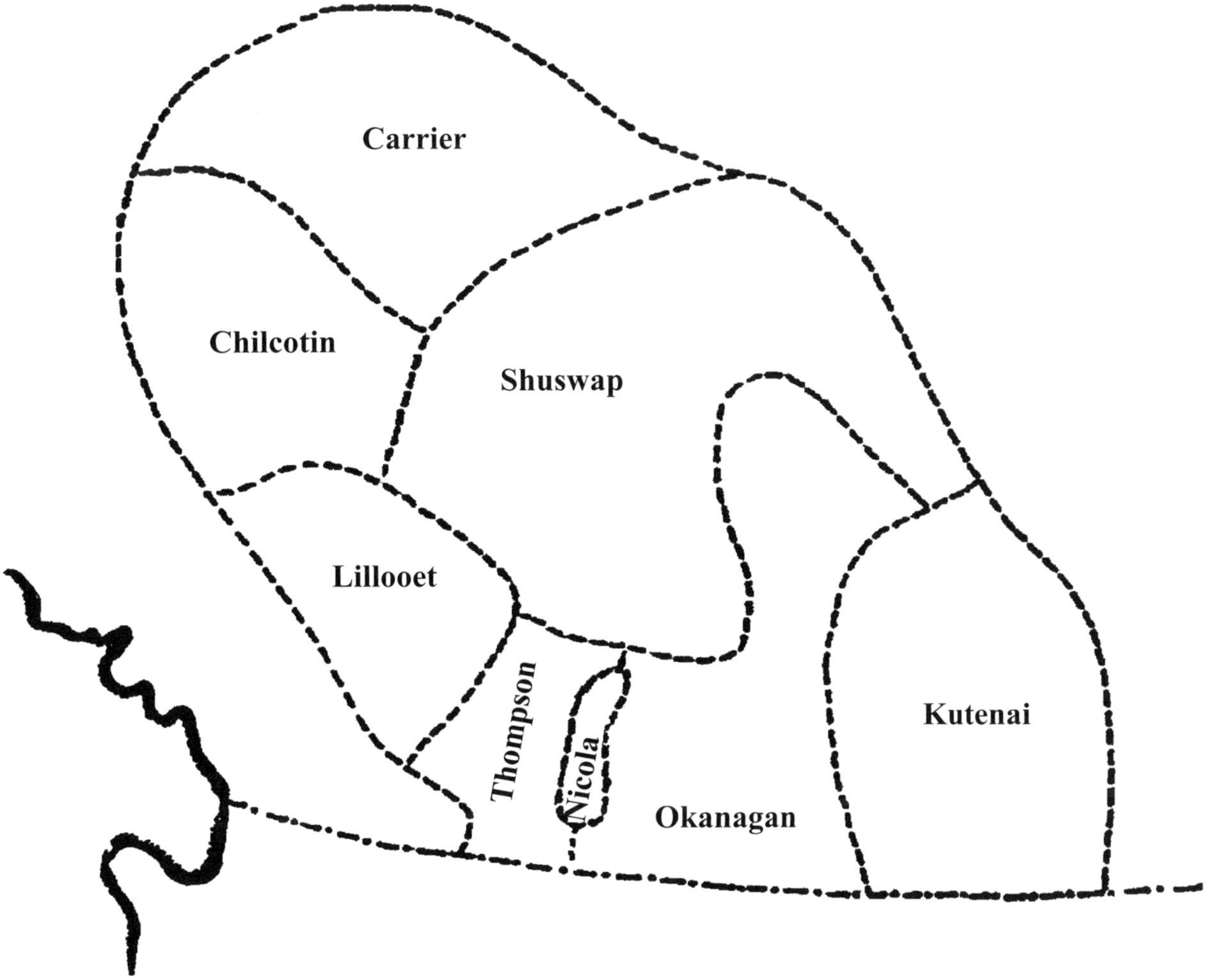

Recommended Resources

Available in most libraries

Ashwell, Reg. *Indian Tribes of the Northwest*. Surrey: Hancock House Publishers Ltd., 1977. Information about specific tribes (Middle to upper grades).

Irwin, R. Stephen M.D. *Hunters of the Sea.* Surrey: Hancock House Publishers Ltd., 1984. Information about hunting methods (Middle to upper grades).

Kalman, Bobbie. *Native Homes*. St. Catharines: Crabtree Press, 2001. Native Nations of North America Series well worth having on your bookshelf (All grades).

Schultz, James Willard. *With the Indians in the Rockies*. Saskatoon, SK, Fifth House Publishers, 1995, first published in 1912. Trapped in the Rocky Mountains in winter. Will the boys survive? Exciting tale by a man who lived with the Blackfoot in the late 1800's. Highly Recommended.

Silvey, Diane. *The Kids Book of Aboriginal Peoples.* Toronto: Kids Can Press, 2005. Great information and full colour paintings. An all inclusive Canadian book (All grades).

Speare, Jean E. (ed.) *The Days of Augusta.* Vancouver; J.J. Douglas Ltd., 1973. Stories from the life of Augusta, a Native woman born in 1888.

Salmon Days

"The salmon! The salmon!" cried Herring Tail, as he and the boys scrambled up the river bank into the village. For a week now the youngsters had run down to the river to look for the first salmon gleaming in the sun as they fought their way upstream.

The cry went through the camp and the village became a hub of excitement. Men checked over their spears and women gathered the nets that had so carefully been mended. The shaman arranged his costume about him. This was his most important hour!

Taking his rattle and basket of eagle down feathers, the shaman stepped carefully from his house. In hushed tones, the village people exclaimed in enthusiasm, as they fell in behind the shaman who marched with slow dignified purpose down the rocky path towards the river. Youngsters were held tightly by the arm so as not to run carefree at this crucial time.

The shaman faced the river with his arms upheld, while the people seated themselves quietly behind him. All must be respectful, because if the spirit of the salmon was displeased, it would not send the fish for the good of the people.

Fearfully, Herring Tail watched the medicine man who danced slowly at first, and then faster and faster, chanting and shaking his rattle. Then he jumped into the air and shook his basket of eagle down feathers; the white fluff tumbled all over him like snow.

The chief's son came forward and the shaman performed some chants over him. The boys couldn't help whispering in awe as the chief's son walked to the platform and stepped out over the tumbling rapids. With expert ease, he dipped his net and scooped a heavy, flopping salmon out of the river. He brought it carefully to the shaman, who had prepared a fire. Clubbing the fish quickly to kill it, the shaman sang a song as he buried it in the coals.

Now came the part of the ceremony that Herring Tail loved best. One after another, the greatest salmon catchers came forward and told stories with dances and songs. They told of how the spirit of the salmon had blessed them with huge gatherings of fish.

Finally the fish was cooked. It was split open and passed around for every villager to take a bite. How good it tasted! Wrapping the bones in a woven mat, the shaman threw them back into the river to release the spirit of the salmon.

Great cheers went up from everyone. It was a good ceremony. The salmon spirit would be pleased. Now they could all gather in the salmon harvest. Herring Tail ran with the boys along the river bank to help gather the fish thrown from the nets. This would be a great salmon year!

The People

In southern British Columbia and southwestern Alberta several mountain ranges run north and south. The Coast Mountains in the west catch the moist air blowing off the ocean. The Rocky Mountains run up the eastern side.

Sandwiched between the coast and the smaller ranges just west of the Rockies is a large rough area called the Interior Plateau.

The plateau is a land of contrasts, with summer meadows next to hilltops of snow. A quiet lake can suddenly become a tumbling, frothy cascade of falls and rapids. This is a rugged land; grim in winter; fatiguing to travel across during the summer.

Here dwelt the Natives of the Plateau, the interior tribes of the west. Abundant animal life and the upstream migrations of salmon each year provided ample food.

> ***Plateau:*** *an extensive land area with a relatively level surface raised above the region surrounding it or at least on one adjacent side.*

The people lived in small groups, moving their camps in spring and fall to be close to the food supply of the season.

David Thompson spent the winter of 1808 trading with the Kutenai of the plateau. Fierce Blackfeet warriors forced him and his men to take their furs east early in the spring. The spring run-off made the country very dangerous for travel. Here are some excerpts about the trip, taken directly from Thompson's journal. This will help you understand the hardships of the plateau.

> On the 28th we set off very early, but soon came to overflowed ground, and had to take to the Mountains climbing up the hills and descending them, to the overflowed pathless woods up to our middle in water, we made slow progress. . .we. . . came to a place where the river was narrow, but the current very strong, . . . we commenced cutting down large Cedars and Pines to fall across the River and form a Bridge to cross on, but the torrent was so rapid, that every tree we threw across the stream was either broken by the Torrent or swept away; as our last hope, a fine Larch of full twelve feet girth, standing twenty four feet from the bank was cut down and fell directly across the River, but in falling the middle of the tree bended and was caught by the rapid current, the head was swept from the opposite bank, the butt end of four feet diameter was carried off the ground, as if it had been a Straw; our last hope being gone, and near noon, we desisted (stopped trying), and with our Horses proceeded up the River to the foot of a steep Hill, ...[1]

[1] Thompson. *Narrative.* p. 391

Project Book
Make a title page for the Natives of the Plateau.

Food

The tribes of the plateau subsisted primarily on the salmon that reached the interior rivers in late summer. This abundant food source was enough to see the natives through the winter months.

The men also hunted bear, beaver, elk and deer. Women were expert diggers and harvested onions and lily roots.

Trade with the coastal tribes or people of the plains offered alternatives in diet.

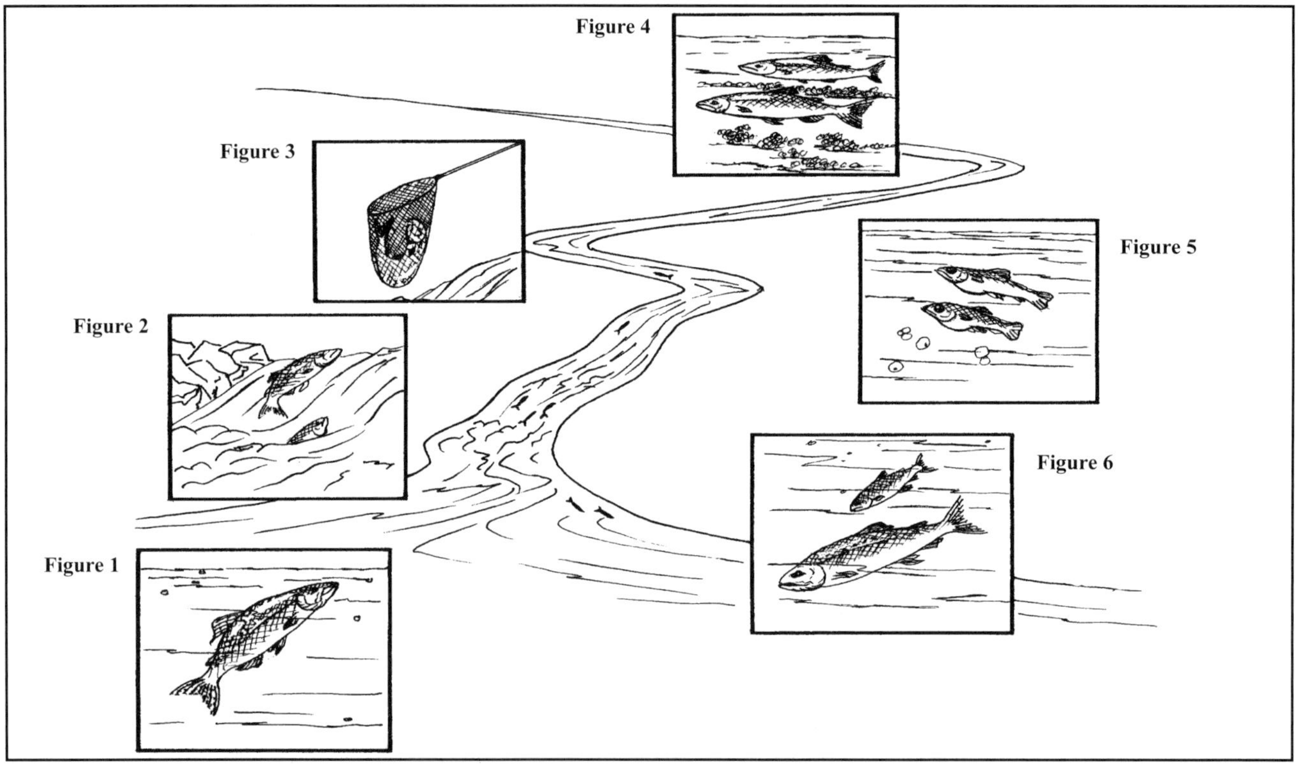

Figures 1 & 2: One of the wonders of nature is the phenomenal return of salmon to the river of their birth. Undaunted by waterfalls and strong currents, the large fish struggle upriver to reach the exact location where they were hatched.

Figure 3: Many dangers await the fish, including hungry animals and fishermen.

Figure 4: Those females that finally make it deposit their eggs, or *spawn*, in nests of gravel (*redd*) in the stream bottom. The male swims alongside fertilizing the eggs.

When the job is completed, the exhausted fish can no longer resist the current. They have not eaten from the time they left the ocean. Weak and dying, they are swept downstream to become food for bears and other scavengers.

Figure 5: The next spring, young salmon, or *parr,* emerge from the eggs. They spend their first year feeding and growing in the freshwater stream.

Figure 6: In the second year, the parr descend with the current down to the sea. For three or four years the developing salmon swim thousands of miles from their original homes, growing rapidly on abundant ocean food.

Suddenly, an inner clock sends the salmon back to that same river. The fish may mill about at the mouth of the river until the water conditions are just right, and then, again, the arduous ascent begins.

Kids Book of Aboriginal Peoples, p. 14-15.

Project Book

Colour the correct project picture of the food of this cultural group. Draw additional pictures and/or write things you learned about the food and the gathering of it. Glue notes and pictures in your project book.

Shelter

In the winter the Natives of the Plateau lived partially underground in pit houses. First, they dug a circle into the ground about one to two meters in depth. The distance across the hole could be up to twelve meters. Above this, pit walls of logs were raised in a cone shape with an opening at the top. The frame, first covered with spruce boughs, was then heaped with dirt. From the outside the home resembled an earthen mound.

The hole in the roof served as both ventilation for smoke and as a doorway. A log notched with steps formed a ladder leading down to the centre of the room. Those entering, would call out to people below to beware of falling dirt.

These homes kept in the heat during winter but were far too damp for summer comfort. In the summer, poles arranged in a cone shape were covered with woven mats or bark much the same as wigwams.

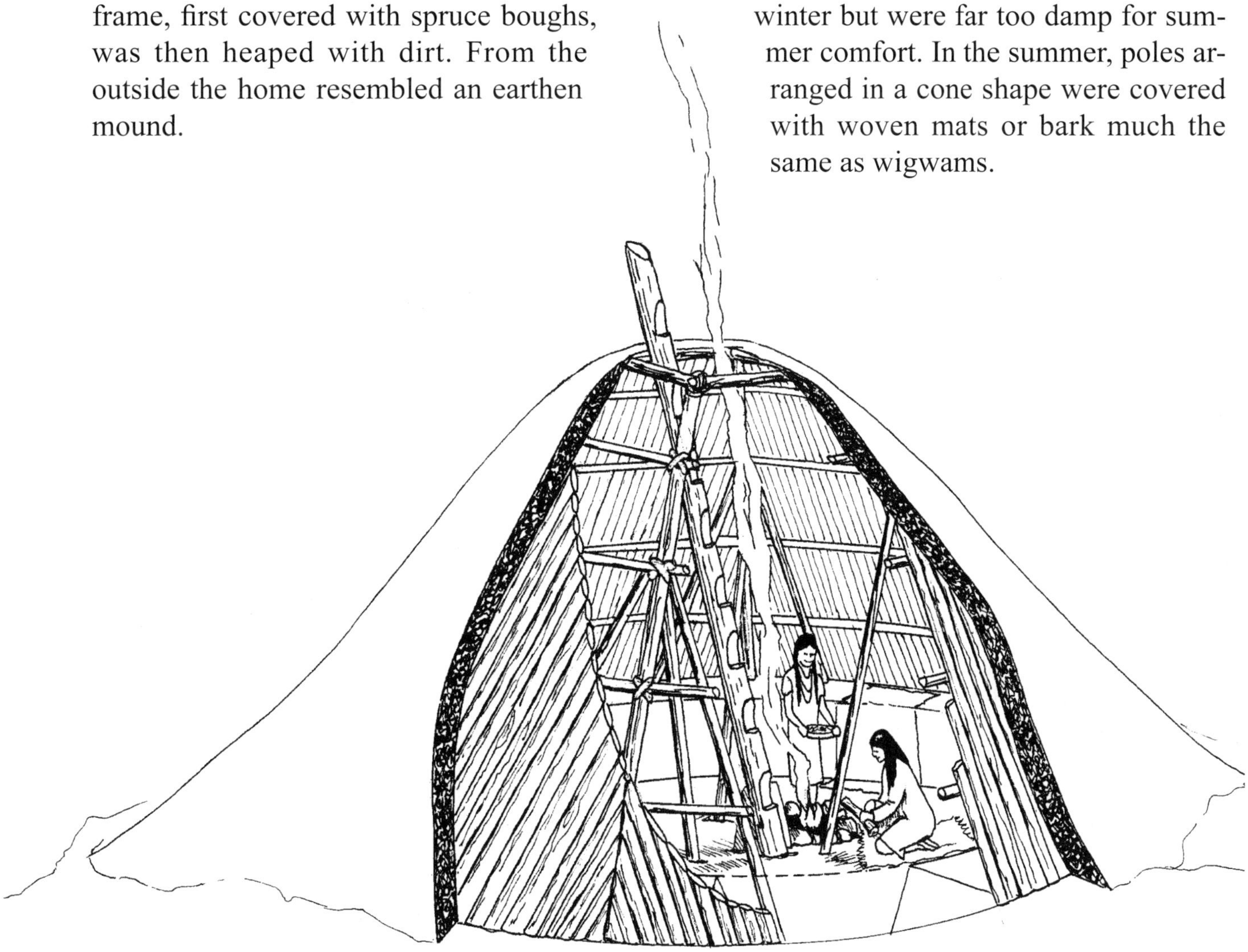

Native Homes, pp. 22-24; Kids Book of Aboriginal Peoples, p. 12-13.

Project Book
Colour the correct project picture of the housing of this cultural group. On lined paper write different things you learned about their shelters. Glue the notes and the picture in your project book.

Moving and Hunting

On the plateau, the best method for moving about was on foot. Canoes were good only for quiet lakes. Most of the rivers were turbulent, tumbling series of waterfalls and rapids. These people often used pack dogs to carry their belongings. In the summer, the people lived near the fishing grounds and berry patches.

Every year the natives could depend on the salmon running up the rivers to spawn. With the reliability of salmon, they did not have to travel as extensively as the subarctic hunters northeast of them. When the fish swam in large numbers up the rivers, men stood on platforms over boiling rapids or waterfalls and scooped the salmon in nets. On more level river banks, they built basket-type traps, or fences called *weirs*. When clustered at the fence, salmon could be scooped with nets or speared.

The men hunted wild game with bows and arrows. In some tribes, the hunters worked cooperatively by beating drums to herd the deer towards hunters. In the summer, the Kutenai tribe ventured onto the plains to hunt the buffalo.

Unlike their neighbours on the northwest Pacific coast, the Natives of the Plateau had furs and clothing made of animal hides. They traded these for fish oil, shells, carved boxes or other goods from the coast.

Here is David Thompson's first-hand account of the salmon run on the Plateau in the early 1800's. Having had poor success in hunting, the men with Thompson had relied on horse meat prior to the arrival of the salmon.

> At length the Salmon made their appearance, and for about three weeks we lived on them. At first they were in tolerable condition, although they had come upwards of twelve hundred miles from the sea, and several weighed twenty five pounds. But as the spawning went upon a gravel bank a short distance above us, they became poor and not eatable. We preferred Horse meat. . . .The Indians affirm, and there is every reason to believe them, that not a single Salmon, of the myriads that come up the River, ever returns to the sea; the shores of the River, after the spawning season, were covered with them, in a lean dying state, yet even in this state, many of the Indians eat them. . . . Salmon. . . speared . . . are split and dried in the smoke, ... When dried by the smoke of Aspin, or other woods of a summer leaf, I have found them good; but dried by the *resinous Wood of the Pine genus, the taste was harsh and unwholesome.[1]

*Pine trees contain resin, a sticky substance used in varnish. Have you ever smelled varnish? Why do you think salmon which was smoked by wood that contained resin tasted bad?

[1] Ibid., p. 377.

Kids Book of Aboriginal Peoples, pp. 16-17.

Project Book
Colour the correct project picture of the method of transportation of this cultural group. Add some notes and glue the notes, project picture and any additional material or pictures in your project book.

Work and Customs

The people of the plateau formed three distinct language groups: the Kutenai, the Athapaskans, and the Salish. The Kutenai may have been people of the plains who were pushed into the mountainous regions by warfare. The northern Chilcotin and Carrier tribes spoke an Athapaskan language similar to their subarctic neighbours. The Salish speaking tribes were the Shuswap, Lillooet, Thompson, and Okanagan.

An outstanding distinction of western tribes was their weaving skills. The women wove waterproof baskets with zigzag patterns and with designs of animals or fish.

The people lived in small groups and did not have an organized system of chiefs or leaders. The wisest man of the band acted as chief when decisions needed to be made.

The tribes of the plateau were greatly influenced by the neighbouring cultures, either the plains or the coastal people.

The interior Salish speaking tribes were aggressive, battling outside tribes and each other. They often took women and children as captives, but rather than making them slaves, they gave them in marriage or adoption.

The more northerly tribes, the Athapaskan speaking people, adopted many of the customs of the subarctic natives to the north.

Project Book
Using a copy of the map from page 4, colour the correct location of this cultural group. Using a copy of the Natives of the Plateau map, colour the locations of the different tribes of this cultural group. Add the maps to your project book.

Activities

Weaving:
Younger children can try weaving a mat using strips of paper.
Older children might make a mat using grasses or rushes available from your area.

Cliff Drawings:
Travellers in central British Columbia have seen mysterious figures on the sides of cliffs painted by Native people long ago. No-one today knows the meanings, however, they may have been done by adolescents during their "vision quest"—a time of solitude when they sought spiritual helpers. Think of a time you have been helped and draw a stick figure scene of the event.

Vocabulary

plateau	*parr*	*weir*
spawn	*weave*	*redd*

Natives of the Plateau Workpage

Answer these questions.

1. The women of the plateau were experts at weaving what item?

____

2. Where was the door in a pit house?

____

3. What fell on people below when someone entered a pit house?

____

4. What are spawn?

____

5. What are parr?

____

Complete this page and add it to your project book.

Natives of the North Pacific Coast

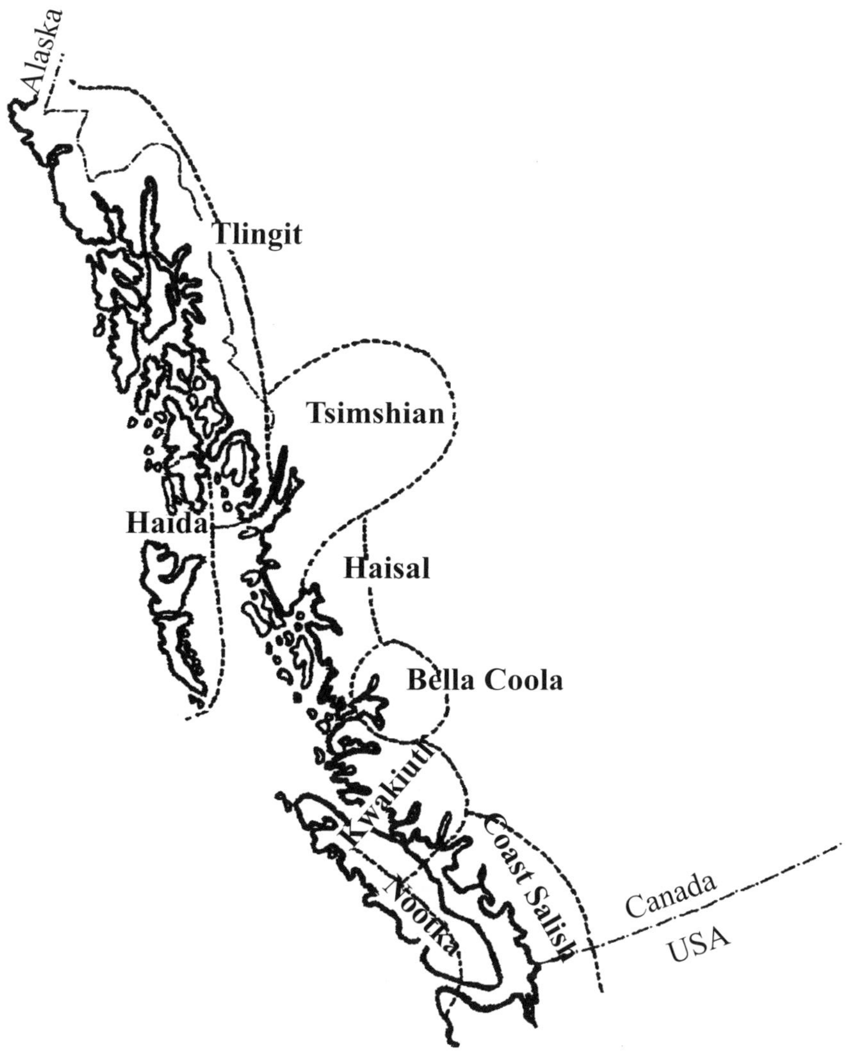

Recommended Resources

Available in most libraries

Cass, James. *Oyai, the Salmon Fisherman and Woodworker.* Indians of the North Pacific Coast. Toronto: D.C. Heath Canada Ltd. and Royal Ontario Museum, 1983. Good for pictures and further information (All grades).

Hirschi, Ron. *Seya's Song.* Seattle: Sasquatch Books, 1992. In this picture book a young Native girl describes her activities on the Northwest Pacific Coast (Early grades).

Holling, C. Holling. *The Book of Indians.* New York: Platt & Munk Co., 1962. Chapters 11-13. These stories were our favourites of the Holling book (All grades).

Irwin, R. Stephen M.D. *Hunters of the Sea.* Surrey: Hancock House Pub. Ltd., 1984. Focuses particularly on hunting and fishing methods (Middle to upper grades).

Jewitt, John R. *White Slaves of the Nootka.* Surrey: Heritage House Pub. Co. Ltd., 1987. First published in 1816. Narrative of the adventures of John R. Jewitt while a captive of the Nootka Indians on Vancouver Island, 1803–1805 (Upper grades).

Kalman, Bobbie. *Nations of the Northwest Coast.* St. Catharines: Crabtree Press, 2001. Native Nations of North America Series well worth having on your bookshelf (All grades).

Kalman, Bobbie. *Native Homes.* St. Catharines: Crabtree Press, 2001. Native Nations of NA (All grades).

Liptak, Karen. *Indians of the Pacific Northwest.* New York: International Book Marketing Ltd., 1991. Lots of good photographs of life today and yesterday (All grades).

McConkey, Lois. *Sea and Cedar. How the Northwest Indians Lived.* Vancouver: Douglas & McIntyre. 1973, 1990. Good for pictures and further information (All grades).

Pearson, Pearle & White, Jenny. *Crests of the Haida.* Vancouver: University of British Columbia. 1985. The stories behind a Haida totem pole (Early to middle grades).

Silvey, Diane. *The Kids Book of Aboriginal Peoples.* Toronto: Kids Can Press, 2005. Great information and full colour paintings. An all inclusive Canadian book (All grades).

Captive

Whale Song shivered in the corner of the strange longhouse. He pressed his hands and feet against the cedar ropes that bound him as he had done time and again, but it was no use, he could not break free. He rocked back and forth in despair.

This disaster was all the more tragic since it was on the eve of his father's potlatch. For months the villagers had worked. Wooden bowls, intricate carved boxes, cedar hats, and robes of sea-otter fur had been prepared. The dancers were carving masks and rehearsing stories.

"I can find you copper," Whale Song had told his father. "Your guests will be astounded at your wealth!"

So it was, four days ago, that Whale Song and his two friends had set out in their canoe. They had travelled up the coast to the inland river where copper had been found before. They had been successful and were on their way home, when enemies had swooped upon them and taken the young men captive.

Whale Song thought of the distress and shame his people would feel when they discovered his capture. As the son of the chief, he was to dance for the final potlatch performance.

The even breathing of those sleeping around him and his own aching muscles lured Whale Song into a fitful stupor. A shuffling sound alerted him and he jumped as someone brushed his arm.

In surprise, he recognized the shadowy form of the chief's daughter. Hours ago, as villagers prodded the captives up the beach, the girl's dark eyes had caught his. For a moment, Whale Song had been lost under her gaze. Now, was she friend or foe?

The cold edge of a stone knife touched Whale Song's hand. He held his breath. Suddenly, his hands were free. After quickly loosening the bonds at his feet, the girl disappeared noiselessly to the shadows of her sleeping mat.

Silently slipping to the door of the longhouse, Whale Song found his bound companions. With thumping heart he fumbled at their ropes and finally freed them.

Frantically they hurried to the water's edge and found their own beached canoe. Pushing off, they began paddling urgently, putting as much distance as possible between them and their captors.

"I will come here again," thought Whale Song. "Instead of revenge, I will bring peace, for I will buy a bride!"

The People

> Whenever a feast is given by the king or any of the chiefs, there is a person who acts as a master of ceremonies, and whose business it is to receive the guests as they enter the house and point out to them their respective seats, which is regulated with great punctiliousness as regards rank; the king occupying the highest or the seat of honour, his son or brother sitting next him, and so on with the chiefs according to their quality;...[1]

John Jewitt, the man who wrote these words, was on the ship called the Boston when she harboured in a bay off Vancouver Island. When the Nootka king, Maquina, attacked and captured the ship, only Jewitt and another man survived. Jewitt lived as Maquina's slave from 1803-1805 until he was rescued. Jewitt's narrative is a window into the lives of Natives of the North Pacific Coast of long ago.

The rugged coast of British Columbia with its forests of gigantic cedar trees, rivers teeming with salmon, and warm coastal temperatures, allowed for large seasonal villages and a more leisurely life than other cultural groups in Canada. There was time for carvers to create huge totem poles or intricate cedar chests. Women wove clothing, blankets, and hats using cedar bark.

One of the most outstanding features of these people was the social classes they had: kings, chiefs, common people and slaves. Great feasts, called Potlatches, displayed a chief's wealth and power to neighbouring tribes.

[1] John R. Jewitt. *White Slaves of the Nootka.* (Surrey: Heritage House Pub. Co. Ltd., 1987), p. 51.

This chief is likely an ancestor of the chief in Jewitt's story.

Chief Maquinna.
A painting by an *18th century* Spanish artist.
Courtesy of B.C. Provincial Archives, used with permission.

Nations of the Northwest Coast, pp 4-7, 20-25; Kids Book of Aboriginal Peoples, p. 6, 8-9

Project Book
Make a title page for the Natives of the North Pacific Coast.

Food

Waves crashed against the beaches and rains drenched the great cedar forests. This was the land of plenty.

The most important resource for all north Pacific coast natives was the salmon that swarmed up the rivers each year to lay its eggs.

Upon entering the river, salmon ceased to eat. Theirs was a relentless struggle against currents, waterfalls and barriers. Why do you think hooks were not effective fishing tools? Instead, spears, nets, traps, and weirs were used. The fish were preserved for winter use by hanging them to dry either in the sun or in the smoky eaves of the longhouses.

Natives of the North Pacific Coast were excellent fishermen. On the ocean, they used hooks and lines as they fished from their dugout canoes for halibut and cod.

Herring, a small fish about 25 cm long, swarmed in the shallows to spawn in early spring. Natives with rakes and nets easily scooped them into canoes. Pine branches weighted down in the water became covered with fish eggs. They were lifted out, sealed in carved tubs and left to *ferment*. This was considered a great delicacy; raw or boiled. Almost all the north Pacific coast people dipped each mouthful of food in fish oil to moisten it. The eulachon fish was so high in oil content that it became valuable not only to those who gathered it, but to the tribes who came to trade for it. The fish was scooped up in spawning runs, and then allowed to spoil in earth pits. The fermented mass was then boiled in a dugout canoe, the oil scooped off and stored in watertight containers.

The Nootka people of Vancouver Island were the only group to actively pursue whales on the rolling seas. The king, or the highest chief present, was always the first to put a harpoon into the whale.

The women gathered a small amount of roots and berries to supplement their diets. Clams, mussels, sea otter, sea lion and seal were also valuable sources of food.

Nations of the Northwest Coast, p. 10; Kids Book of Aboriginal Peoples, p. 11.

Project Book
Colour the correct project picture of the food of this cultural group. Draw additional pictures and/or write things you learned about the food and the gathering of it. Glue notes and pictures in your project book.

Shelter

Along with the harvest of the sea, cedar was important, providing everything necessary for shelter, clothing, and tools. From these huge trees the natives constructed their large plank homes capable of housing many families.

First, permanent frames were built with huge corner posts. Planks were made by splitting cedar logs with wooden wedges and stone hammers. These planks were slipped into the frame in such as way as to be easily removed. When a family travelled to their summer fishing village, they transported the planks, leaving a skeleton frame village.

Relatives lived together. The most important family slept farthest from the doorway. Family spaces were divided by cedar chests and woven mats. The highest chief owned the biggest home in the village. This house was also a meeting place. During celebrations, family dividers were cleared back to make room for invited guests.

Food was cooked on indoor fire pits. Sometimes a roof board was slipped back to allow the smoke to escape, but more often, the smoke was left to circulate around the eaves, drying the many fish hanging there.

A *totem* is an animal associated with a clan. The people believed this animal was their sacred ancestor and protector. In front of the homes, totem poles proudly guarded the village. The carved figures of animals each had a story behind it. Some figures often used were the bear, the raven, or the killer whale. Some tribes used their totems as doorposts with a hole carved in the bottom that became the entrance into the house.

Native Homes, pp. 28-29; Nations of the Northwest Coast, pp 12-13; Kids Book of Aboriginal Peoples, p. 7.

Project Book

Colour the correct project picture of the housing of this cultural group. On lined paper write different things you learned about their shelters. Glue the notes and the picture in your project book.

Travel and War

The sea not only provided bountiful food but became the highway for travel. With much skill and hard labour, canoes were hollowed from cedar logs. They were designed to easily handle rolling ocean swells. Large dugout canoes, often elaborately carved and decorated, could carry forty to fifty men.

The smaller canoes were used when the men went fishing and hunting for sea mammals along the coast.

Pacific coast natives, painted and fierce, went in their large canoes to raid far away tribes. They killed the men and captured the women and children as slaves. The village was then plundered for goods such as copper, furs, or blankets. Slaves were valued because the number owned by a chief denoted wealth. Slaves lived as one of the family and were treated well, although their work load was heavy.

Trade became important to the point that some tribes specialized in certain skills such as basket-making or blanket-weaving. Fish oil was so desired by the Natives of the Plateau, that paths to the interior were called "grease trails."

In the following selection, Jewitt describes some trading parties.

> Whenever they came to visit or trade . . . (they would). . . stop a few miles distant under the lee of some bluff or rock, and rig themselves out in their best manner by painting and dressing their heads (with goose down) . . . .
>
> . . . whenever they wished to purchase any particular object, as for instance a certain slave. . . the canoe that came for this purpose would lie off at a little distance from shore. A. . . representative . . . after making . . . a pompous speech, (would) hold up specimens of . . . articles . . . to offer in payment, ... If the bargain was concluded the exchange was immediately made.[1]

[1] Ibid., pp. 65, 66.

Nations of the Northwest Coast, pp 18-19; Kids Book of Aboriginal Peoples, p. 10.

Project Book

Colour the correct project picture of the method of transportation of this cultural group. Add some notes and glue the notes, project picture and any additional material or pictures in your project book.

Work and Customs

The most outstanding custom of the Natives of the Northwest Pacific Coast was the *Potlatch.* The feast was given in honour of a special occasion such as a totem raising, a marriage, or a daughter coming to marriageable age. The chief's status amongst other tribes was confirmed or raised by the quality of the event.

For months, even years, the villagers would prepare for the feast making gifts, masks for dancing, and food. Up to five hundred guests might be invited and the feasting could go on for several days. Songs and dances performed by the hosting tribe, told stories of a family's history, and proclaimed fishing and hunting rights.

Potlatch means gift. The chief was expected to bestow on his guests some of his wealth. The greater the gifts, the greater his rank and honour. Canoes, slaves, blankets, tools and ornaments were given away; the best to the most important guests. Each tribe would try to outdo the previous *potlatch.*

Since the climate at the Pacific coast is warmer than other places in Canada, most often the natives needed no clothes. Skirts and cloaks were not made of animal hide, as the clothing of other native groups, but were woven from cedar roots and bark. Blankets, often a mixture of bark and goat or dog hair, were woven on large looms. Unique to this cultural group were the woven cedar hats which protected people from the continuous rain. A chief's hat could be very elaborate.

The Pacific coast natives were fond of decorating themselves - the men, more so than the women. They wore nose rings, ear rings, and painted their faces. For festive occasions or visits, the men oiled their hair, gathered it and tied it on top of their heads. Their heads were then covered with white goose down. They were very particular not to have a single feather out of place.

Says Jewitt of Chief Maquinna:

> Though the women, as I have said, make but little use of paint, the very reverse is the case with the men. . . . I have known Maquinna after having been employed for more than an hour in painting his face, rub the whole off and recommence the operation anew when it did not entirely please him. . . .
>
> On extraordinary occasions, the king and principal chiefs used to strew over their faces, after painting, a fine black shining powder, procured from some mineral. . . .This . . . they . . . value . . . . highly, as, in their opinion, it serves to set off their looks to great advantage, glittering, especially in the sun, like silver.[1]

[1] Ibid., pp. 54–55.

Project Book
Using a copy of the map from page 4, colour the correct location of this cultural group. Using a copy of the Natives of the Pacific Coast map, colour the locations of the different tribes of this cultural group. Add the maps to your project book.

Activities

Totem pole:
Make a family totem pole using a roll from kitchen wrap or gift wrap. Think of some animal symbols that might represent your family, such as pets or the wild animals in favourite vacation spots. Draw patterns and use paint or construction paper to design your totem. Pictures of totem poles in books might give you some ideas.

Throw a potlatch:
At Home:
1. Ask your parents if you can have friends over. Discuss the following ideas with them.
2. Find some things you could give away as gifts, such as paperbacks you won't read again, hockey cards, little toys, etc. Check with your parents about your items. (They might be glad for you to clean the junk out of your room!)
3. Make some treats for your guests to eat. They might not like fermented fish eggs, or dried salmon; so, cupcakes or cookies would be good.
4. Plan entertainment. Natives of the Pacific Coast had dances, skits and stories. If you think your friends would like that, do it. Otherwise, games are always enjoyable.
5. Tell your friends you are studying the Natives of Canada. Describe what you have learned about a potlatch. Tell them not to bring a gift. At this party they will receive gifts instead. Ahead of time, choose the gift that would please each friend.
6. Throw a potlatch party!

At School:
1. Plan a potlatch party with your teacher.
2. Decide how to choose someone to be chief (ie. the oldest in the class, or draw straws etc.)
3. In groups, plan three or four skits to act out stories. Make costumes and masks.
4. On party day, everyone should bring in goodies and an item from home that can be given away as a gift.
5. Set up a special chair for the chief and pile all the gifts around it.
6. After the entertainment, the chief passes out the gifts and the feasting begins.

Vocabulary

ferment	*18th century (1700's)*
potlatch	*totem*

Natives of the Pacific Coast Workpage

1. Put the food items below in the proper column. Were they obtained by gathering, hunting, or fishing?

whale **cod** **fish eggs**
salmon **berries** **sea otter**
roots **sea lion** **halibut**

GATHERED	HUNTED	FISHED

2. Men carved with wood, and women wove various items from cedar bark. Put 4Ethe appropriate items in the proper column.

hat **food box** **basket**
canoe **cape** **mat**
blanket **bowl** **ladle**
totem pole **skirt** **spear**

CARVED	WOVEN

Complete this page and add it to your project book.

Project Resources and Workpages Answer Key

Student Notebook

The student's Natives of Canada project book should include the following:

- Title page (title, student's name, student's grade or age, date completed)
- Table of Contents (completed at end of project when pages are numbered)
- Seven sections for each of seven cultural groups
- Maps (7 copies of p. 4, 1 copy each Unit heading map)
- Workpages (at end of each Unit)
- Project Pictures
- Folder or envelope for storage of pictures until used.

Early grade students should just classify the project pictures. Middle grade children could label and write notes with each picture. Upper grade students may add research notes and a bibliography.

Food

Shelters

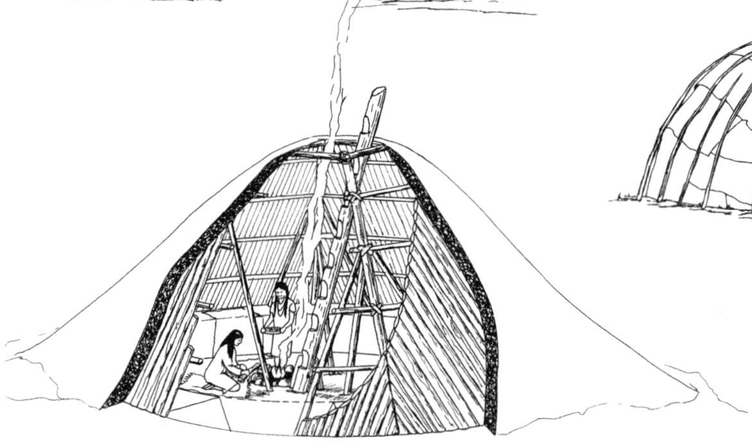